Title

Errors of Ignorance
Part 1

Walter L. Crider, Author

Table of Contents

Prologue
We are within ourselves and only us to know.

Erich Fromm

Another rainy day, Saturday in June, 1932. The swollen dark clouds hanging low still spilling more into streams already overflowing their banks, puddles everywhere and the red-clay road ruts and ditches filled. Not a travel day, especially by cars. Clyde had our mule, Pat, hitched to the one-horse buggy. Rain curtains snapped in. I was ready with rain coat and rubber overshoes. Clyde urged Pat to go, and we two started the 10-mile trip to the train station in Chatham. The front rain curtain and dash board kept the splashing mud from Pat's trotting hooves out, and the side curtains kept us mostly dry.

Not much conversation between an eight-year-old boy and a 20-year-old, married hired man. We just rode, with Clyde speaking to Pat to keep her in the best part of the road. No other traffic until we got to the paved road at the train station. We got there and parked under a shed roof only a short time before the train stopped to let my daddy off. Clyde put Daddy's suit case in the covered back trunk, and the three of us started the return home. Clyde and Daddy talked some.

This was a bi-weekly trip from Baltimore where Daddy had a job with the Federal Land Bank. The bank that he had worked for in Danville had gone bankrupt, and he had closed out the accounts, mostly with the Baltimore bank, in such an efficient way that he was offered a position there. The severe financial depression caused a lot of emotional depression too. It also offered challenges of survival that tested resourcefulness. Daddy needed money to buy his ancestral farm from his two sisters, but the farm had no financial value. Mother's Chatham

3

property could be used as collateral for a loan. They exchanged property, and Mother and we three younger children moved to the farm and stayed there while Daddy worked in Baltimore making enough money to pay off the mortgage.

I did not have much contact with my daddy during his life. He was mostly a visitor in our home. Saved for financial support, discipline and vacations. All of which he generously provided. He seldom talked about his parents or his life experiences. He was a man within himself. Guided by his life experiences, some of which were so deeply hidden in his memory that he did not know they existed. Still, they were part of who he was as a person and they controlled his thoughts and behavior.

I was the youngest of his five children who lived to adulthood and probably the one who lived closest to him emotionally during my adult years. I had some reasonably close ideas of what stored experiences made him the person he was. However, not until late in my life did I begin to get a better understanding of his and my psychological being.

My brother, Paul expressed himself: *Daddy was a very remarkable – and troubled – man who had great personal fortitude, determination, intelligence, character and integrity and one who surmounted numerous and great obstacles which would have stopped lesser men dead in their tracks.*

I only wish that I could have known him – and he me – don't you wish the same?

It would have made the lives of his children less troubled if we had known him better, and, if he had known himself, it may have made his life and his children's lives very different.

Chapter 1

Early Influences

Creon's speech in Sophocles' "Antigone":

"So it is right my son, to be disposed

in everything to back your father's quarrel.

It is for this men pray to breed and rear

In their homes dutiful offspring—to requite

The foe with evil, and their father's friendship

Honor, as did their father. Whoso gets

Children unserviceable—what else could he

Be said to breed, but troubles for himself,

And store of laughter for his enemies"

Edgar Palmer Crider, Jr. was not the first human on this earth. He had a lot of kin people already here, and he had a lot of deceased ancestors for hundreds of years past. All of his ancestors had some influence on what his physical body was, and everyone else had an influence on the kind of world he would live in. The most influential were those nearest to him: the genealogical ancestors back at least to his great grandparents, the nearest neighbors and social and environmental contacts.

Parental grandparents were John Wesley and Emma Palmer Crider. He an orphan boy of about four or five years old when he was taken in by a Methodist Preacher, Jehu Hanks. A question to me is the source of his middle name, John *Wesley* Crider since there were none of his family members with that name. I suspect John's original name was changed to John Wesley by Mr. Hanks as a common custom of changing one's sinful life into one of Christian godliness and honoring much admired deceased Christian leaders. John's original name was lost to history and not traceable to his birth parents.

Edgar, Jr.'s ancestors settled in the northwest area of Pittsylvania County, Virginia in a community known as Toshes. Because my great grandfather, John Wesley Crider (born 4-14-1831, died 2-28-1906) was an orphan, I have not been able to trace his ancestry with reliable records. The records of other Criders in the Toshes area before the birth date of my great grandfather start with Daniel Crider (Kreider) (born 1744 in Pennsylvania). He was the son of John Michael Kreider (born 1712 in Germany) and was 20 years old when he arrived in Philadelphia 8-11-1732. died 7-?-1761). Daniel Crider married Catherine Berger in Pennsylvania before 1766. In looking at recorded births, marriages and deaths from this union available to me up through the time when my great grandfather was born, I have found that Daniel and Catherine had 10 sons and one daughter. The two youngest were born in Toshes, Virginia, and the others were born in Pennsylvania. Their son, John William (born 1777, died 1834), had two sons most nearly matching the probable adult dates and ages when my great grandfather, John Wesley Crider, was born. Either John William, Jr. (born 1809, died after 1860) or Jacob (born 1809, died 1874) and who were 25 years old in 1834 appear to me to have probably been my great grandfather's father. The recorded information shows that John William, Jr. had no children, so my best guess is that Jacob and his wife Nancy Rohrer (born 12-14-1814, died 6-? -1839) were his parents and named him John William for his uncle and grandfather. One inconsistency with my guess is that the recorded marriage date that I found is: 12-19-1832, and my great grandfather's birth date is recorded 4-

14-**1831** and **1834.** The latter appears more likely since it is a more recent record during his life. Nancy's death date is consistent with the time when my great grandfather became an orphan.

He would have been either 4 or 5 years old. Also, it is recorded that his father, Jacob, died in Crittenden County, Kentucky.

Transcribed from a publication of the Methodist Episcopal Church South, Virginia Conference:

Rev. John Wesley Crider

The venerable Jehu Hank, now of the Baltimore conference, took a fatherless boy of Pittsylvania County, Virginia, reared and educated him. The orphan became a minister, and on his first circuit as a junior participated in a Pentecostal revival, where 900 were converted. Mr. Crider loves to tell of the kindness of this noble Christian minister and his devoted wife, always affirming they should have the praise for any good that he may do in life. Mr. Crider joined the church as a seeker, after deep conviction of sin, at the age of 10, and was converted four years afterward. When approaching manhood, he went south and prepared for the ministry under a divine call to that vocation. He joined the South Carolina Conference at Columbia on December 16, 1854. For 17 years he continued a member of that body, with success attending his labors, and in some instances, great display of grace were manifested on his work. In 1871 he succumbed to the southern fevers, and, by medical advice, sought the latitude of Piedmont Virginia. He returned to his native county of Pittsylvania, where he was born April 1834 and rested during 1872. In 1873 he formed the East Franklin circuit, and was transferred to the Virginia conference. In 1874 he was assigned to the

Henry circuit, and continues in active service among us. In the 35 years of his ministerial labors Mr. Crider has quit him well of his charges. His social qualities and efficiency in the pulpit give him success.

He is in height about 5 feet five; in weight, ranging between 130 and 135; in complexion, fair; light hair and blue eyes. The amiable qualities of heart and spirituality of life can be seen in the earnestness of his honest, truthful face. His voice is pleasant and clear; forcible-- thoroughly understood by all; his gestures, without effort, natural and easy; his mind, elevated and ennobled by an integrity established in sincerity and fortified by religion; his general manner, dignified, earnest and thoughtful; truth and sincerity shine throughout his whole conduct; in disposition, loving and kind; of liberal views and sympathetic nature, yet possessed of a firmness and decision of character unsurpassed in resisting anything that involves the principles of honor and truth, and any impeachment of his own religious principles and unblemished character is sure to meet with a quick and righteous rebuke. He has convictions and is not afraid of them; speaks as a commissioned teacher, with the zeal of conviction and the authority of innocence. He is self-reliant and uncomplaining--never asking favors, but most grateful for sympathy when received.

His sermons abound in the most sublime truths, with the most exalted sentiments of piety and devout gratitude; his illustrations are remarkable for introducing the best lessons from incidental objects and occasions; his prayers alone, so effectual and fervent in spirit, are a benediction.

Loved and respected by all good people, they feel, indeed, that he

is with them in the spirit of the Lord when he says," I am your servant. for
Jesus sake." Eternity alone will reveal the vast amount of good of this
most faithful and consecrated worker.

John Wesley joined the Methodist Church as a seeker at age 10
and as a member at age 14. Sometime after that he went to South
Carolina and joined the SC Methodist Conference 12-16-1854. While
living in SC he was ordained a Methodist minister, and he married Emma
Hortense Palmer of Marion, SC (born 8-29-1835; died 1-6-1919). Their
children, my grandfather, Edgar Palmer (born 9-12-1859, died 2-19-
1908), John Oscar (born 11-23-1861, died 4-10-1926), Bessie (born 1863,
died 1959), Stella and Mamie probably were also born in South Carolina.
In 1871 he contracted the "southern fevers" (maybe malaria?) and for
health reasons he returned to the Piedmont latitude in Virginia near
Toshes. After a year of recuperating, in 1873 he formed the East Franklin
Circuit and was transferred to the Virginia Conference

Sometimes Edgar traveled with his father on his circuit-riding
church visits, one of which was Olive Branch Methodist church near
where the Anderson, Smith and Cook families and farms were located.
This was significant because Louisa Anderson was a "maiden" lady of 21
who often visited her older sister, Susan, who had married James Cook in
1886. They were members of Olive Branch Methodist Church where
John Wesley visited two times each month as pastor to three churches in
his circuit. On most visits he brought his son Edgar, also 21, and they had
a late noon meal at the Cook house before returning to their home at
Toshes about 6 miles away. Louisa attended church meetings with her
sister's family and enjoyed the meal social time. An attraction between

9

Edgar and Louisa, (born 8-14-1859, died 4-12-1908), developed, and they were married September 12, 1880 by Edgar"s father in the Anderson home.

Louisa's father, Watt Otey, as a marriage gift, gave Louisa the use of a house and small farm where they lived during her father's life time and continued to live there until her mother died in 1889. Louisa then inherited the farm of about 200 acres from her father, but, because women were not legally allowed to own property, it was held in trust by her oldest brother, James.

Children came. Five years between births and a burden for Louisa. Even with a small house, three children and meager food, Louisa had her mother live with her during a short time before her death.

Edgar Palmer Crider, Junior was born into a family of meager financial resources, but with plentiful love and caring. A three-room log cabin with mother, father and five-year-old sister, Nancy.

I did not have much contact with my daddy during his life. He was mostly a visitor in our home. Saved for financial support, discipline and vacations. All of which he generously provided. He seldom talked about his parents or his life experiences. My brother, Paul, transcribed the hand-written account he made describing the early part of his life.

Below is a copy of Paul's transcription of what Daddy wrote.

I was born in Pittsylvania County, Virginia on June 12, 1888. My mother was a Louisa Craft Anderson, daughter of Otey Watt Anderson and Nancy Smith Anderson. My father was Edgar Palmer Crider son of

Early Influences

John Wesley Crider and Emma Palmer Crider.

My mother was born on August 14, 1859; my father on September 12, 1859. They were married on September 12, 1880. My father died on February 19, 1908, and my mother died April 12, 1908. Both are now buried in my family plot in the town cemetery of Chatham, Virginia

My oldest sister, Nancy Emma Crider, was born July 18, 1883; I was born June 12, 1888, and my youngest sister, Mary Louise was born on February 1, 1894.

Both of my maternal grandparents died before I was born. My grandmother Anderson was left a widow and lived the last few years of her life with my parents.)

The Andersons were large landowners in Callands Magisterial district in Pittsylvania County, Virginia – their lands lay along Tomahawk and Keesee creeks. Their old homestead was situated on Tomahawk Creek where my mother and her sisters and brothers were raised.

My grandmother Anderson was determined to give all of her children a college education. My mother attended Roanoke Female College in Danville Virginia – it is now Averett College. My grandmother Anderson lived with my mother and father awhile before she died; both Anderson grandparents are buried in the Anderson Cemetery which is located on part of the land that I now own.

Grandmother Anderson was determined that all of her children receive a good education, and she succeeded in this to a large extent: Uncle Charles Anderson graduated from Richmond College, Uncle John from the Medical School in Richmond, uncle Edward attended Virginia Military Institute and then went on to the United States Military Academy at West Point, New York, from which he graduated, and Uncle George graduated from Richmond College, also. Her eldest son, my Uncle James, had to assume full responsibility of supervising and managing the farms and of providing all of the expenses of educating his sister and brothers, so he did   did not have the opportunity, as his sister and brothers, so he did not have the opportunity as had the others, to attend college. He built Anderson's Mill on Tomahawk Creek and operated it until his death.

At grandmother Anderson's death my mother inherited her home and adjoining land, which consisted of about 150 acres, and the small farm along Keesee Creek, consisting of about 50 acres, both totaling about 200 acres of land. On the home place there was a house, with one room downstairs and one upstairs, and with a shed for a cook room. This house was about a half-mile from the public road – known as the Anderson Mill Road, and which is now road number 649 – and was close to a good running branch and a good running spring of water. To the west of this house was a one-room log cabin on top of a hill, on the same branch but near another goods spring of water.

On the small farm (about 50 acres) there was a one-room log cabin with a shed room. This house was occupied by a Colored tenant-farmer who lived there 18 years and raised a family of nine children. He had one mule, a wagon, a few plows and some small tools, and paid my mother one-fourth of his crops each year. His name was Alfred Moorman (he had a son named Vaden Moorman who, among other business activities, later operated his own cab in and around Chatham and the County generally) and his wife was Henrietta. They were good people, and most of their children turned out well.

After we three children came along, my mother tried to arrange to build a home up from the bottom to the public road. Uncle James Anderson, in addition to his corn and wheat mill, operated a sawmill and agreed to cut the tumbler from Mother's land for the new house and build it for her for $300. After trying the bank in Chatham and individuals, she found that she could not borrow this amount. Uncle Jim then agreed to build the house for her and give her time to pay him out of the rent she received from her farms. After having made these arrangements for the new house, she rented the farms and agreed for the tenant to move into the house we were then living in. Due to the slow progress in building the new house, we had to move into the cabin on the hill in order to give the incoming tenant possession of the house we were living in as agreed. We lived there for a year until we moved into the new house – in 1894 or '95.

I should mention that when I was born they had great trouble in finding food that was agreeable to me – I was so delicate. I breast-fed two white women in the community and one Colored woman, all of whom had babies about my age.

It was while living in the cabin that my great-grandmother Crider, who owned a small farm at Climax, became too ill to live alone (she was 90), so mother took her to live with us in the cabin where she stayed for several months before she died. We didn't have much to share with her – just a little food and loving care. It was on Christmas Night in this cabin that I awoke and heard Mama sobbing because Santa had left so little in the stockings by the fireplace. In later years I had this cabin moved to the back lot of the home situated on the highway. It was repaired and made very convenient and comfortable for summer use.

Our first years at school we attended a one-room school situated about 2 miles from home, known as Tomahawk School. To get to the school, we traveled the farm road through the lower farm and over a path through fields and woods the balance of the way (which was also used by Abner and Berkley Mahan and by Uncle Jim and Uncle Charlie Anderson's children. My father felled a tree across Keesee Creek as a means for us to cross it. If it was too wet or slippery we would have to straddle it and "coon" our way over to keep from falling into the creek.

Public schools were generally for the early grades, limited in facilities, of frame or log construction, heated by a wood-burning heater, with a small toilet situated some distance away. The boys were assigned to cut wood and supply the heater. Being one room, the atmosphere for study was, as a rule, difficult. In my few years at the school we had some very fine teachers. Miss Lulu Pearson was my first teacher and she was a kind and gentle person. Then I had as my teacher Miss Blanche Haynes. All of the students were in the same room for the first year or two. Later, another room was added and the students in the higher grades were transferred there, and all of the students were adjusted accordingly. When I was 12 years old I looked around for a job in a store. For several years, I had helped neighbors harvest their tobacco crops, holding sticks for the cutters, working by the day for a wage of .25 cents a day and board. A work day then was from sun up until sometime after dark. Then I would walk home with a quarter in my hand!

My notes

Though not remembered, Jr. was given an emotional feeling of love that remained a part of his life. Initial unremembered mother love supplemented by later mother and family love started Jr.'s psychological life.

As was the custom, all babies and very young children, boys and girls, were dressed in washable cloth diapers and dresses. Young Edgar was dressed that way until he was almost three and beginning to retain and recall the memories of his experiences: the beginning of himself as a person. His father, mother and older sister doted on him as a loved and treasured son and brother. No bad memories to haunt him. Self-worth to give him confidence as a person of value. No concept of poverty, just acceptance of his life as it was. No comparisons to evaluate.

No memory of his fragile condition clinging to life. Racial prejudice was the social custom and the law, but not always practiced. A black lady, Louisa Craft, willingly and lovingly nursed Jr. as her own, and Jr.'s mother accepted with gratitude her gift of life for her adored baby. Not so much an exception to the social custom, but one not openly admitted.

Edgar, Jr. started with no memory of any experiences, just the ability to start accumulating them and, thus, becoming a psychological person. His experiences with his physical surroundings were gradually expanded as he grew older. His family and later his social surroundings formed his changing psychological person. The social attitudes and customs of family and neighbors were what was available to Edgar, Jr., and it shaped and drove his entire life.

Edgar raised a garden, did some house repairs, cut firewood and did some home outside work. After the annual tenant's money paid the local store bill, Edgar spent what little income the tenant farmers produced.

Edgar Junior loved his father and understood the true reason for his addiction to whiskey and opium, but he was ashamed of his father's reputation in the community. Life was what he experienced. Some of these experiences were remembered later in his life when he did have more experiences to compare them with. Then realizing the tenuous life he and his family had lived. A frail boy child, a loving mother, a five-years older supporting sister, Nancy, and a father unsuited for and physically unable to live the life available to him. No paternal family for support, but lots of maternal family for support and criticism of his father. Little Edgar grew into child hood and beyond to school age. Learning to help around the house and garden.

During several conversations with Daddy while I was growing up and as a mature man, he told me about his father having a dislocated left shoulder that caused him great pain. He had said that the shoulder was out of joint from childhood wrestling and no one had been able to permanently put it back. It always slipped back out of joint causing intolerable pain when moved. He wanted to do more on the farm and around the house, but could not consistently do so. Daddy had seen his father struggle with work around the house and garden and also trying to farm using two mules. He tried to only use his right arm while cutting and splitting wood and harnessing and hitching up the mules. Trying to plow using only his right arm. All the time showing intense pain. It was not for show to convince anyone, but Daddy could see the real pain and his father's tears as he tried and tried again to be a farmer. He just couldn't do

16

it. Junior knew that it was real, not to convince anyone. There was no one around to convince. Junior could almost feel the pain himself, and he loved his father for his efforts. Grandmother saw the pain and loved him for his efforts and loved him for his pains. She suffered also from the attitude and belief of her family members that it was all just an excuse to justify his use of whiskey and opium. They controlled the church, and they influenced the attitude of neighbors against Grandfather.

Junior helped with household chores, vegetable gardening and working for other farmers for 25 cents a day during tobacco planting and harvesting seasons. He also had another chore when he was 10 years old. Being sent by his mother about three miles to the local ordinary at Redeye to bring his father home. Junior enjoyed his other productive chores, but he hated this one. His mother hated it too and was fearful that these experiences at such a young age would forever become a way of life for her adored son. She would wait until she was desperate for help. Sometimes for lack of firewood or a pig out of the pen that needed repair. She did not send Junior lightly but from desperation and a heavy heart. He walked with dread and some fear along the three miles of dirt road. Always in the evening hours when there were the most customers and boisterous activity. Loose women, trollops, wenches and women of ill repute in general were hanging onto whiskey-drinking men. Talking, drinking, staggered dancing and slurred singing to string music. Jr. tried to enter unnoticed, quickly find his father and leave with him, but that never happened. A ten-year old boy did not go unnoticed in there. He steeled his nerve and determination to fulfill his mission. His father was never ready to leave and prolonged their stay. Grandfather loved his son and never abused him physically or mentally. They walked home in silence.

After several warnings and repentances, the Greenpond Church Board of Deacons expelled Edgar, Sr. from membership in the Church. Louisa resigned.

There was no happy ending for Edgar senior. Just physical pain and mental anguish from the attitude of his wife's family and neighbors. He loved his family, and was very sorry for his inability to care for them and for the disgrace that his affliction had brought to them. The facts were irrefutable. He was worthless to anyone including himself. His only way to continue living was to drown his pain and mental anguish through the use of mind-numbing drugs of whiskey and opium. Both legal and easily available; for a price.

Use of both of these drugs caused him to be addicted and appear as only a worthless scoundrel. Junior had seen the results of pain relief for his father and the social attitude toward him as a willful worthless drug addict. Even though his daddy was thought by everyone who knew him to be a worthless scoundrel, Junior knew him to honestly suffer pain during his efforts to farm and do work around the house. There was mutual love between the two, but his father's efforts to cope with his pain through whiskey and opium only intensified negative opinions about him. The only way Junior thought of to help was to find work to help pay for family needs and for his father's addictive drugs.

Paul's transcription continues:

When I was 12 years old I looked around for a job in a store. For several years, I had helped neighbors harvest their tobacco crops, holding sticks for the cutters, working by the day for a wage of .25 cents a day and board. A work day then was from sun up until sometime after dark. Then I would walk home with a quarter in my hand!

Aunt Mamie Ashlin, my father's sister who lived in Norfolk, Virginia, wrote mother that she and my uncle (her husband) could give me a job in their small grocery store which was located at the corner of Bute and Bremer streets in Norfolk, Virginia. She said that they would pay me one dollar and a half per week and give me board. So, in 1901 (I was about 13 years old then), mother sold pork sausage and bought enough cloth to make me a pair of pants and a coat for me to leave home in.

My notes:

Much later, when I was small, Daddy's older sister, Aunt Nancy said that in addition to and a much greater reason that their Aunt Mamie and Uncle Ed offered Junior a job in Norfolk was that their mother was at her wits end with fear of the bad influence and social reputation of his father would have on Jr.

In 1901 when Daddy was 12, Louisa gathered her courage and asked her sister in law, Mamie Ashlin, to give Daddy a home and job in her husband's, Edward's, grocery store in Norfolk, VA. More than 200 miles and far away from his father and her family. To give him a sense of responsibility, he was told that he was going to make money for himself and to send some home to his mother, and he never knew differently.

Paul's transcription continues:

I got a ride to Chatham and took the train to Danville and, at 3 o'clock the next morning, took the train to Norfolk – arriving at Pinner's Point about dark, and transferred to a ferryboat for the city of Norfolk. Grandfather Crider was supposed to meet me on the boat, but somehow missed me, but I found a seat and waited. When the boat was ready to start, it gave a great whistle blast right under me and liked to have scared me to death. About that time grandpa found me and I was much relieved.

Upon arrival at the dock in Norfolk, we took a streetcar, the first one I had ever seen, and rode home to 444 Bute St. where I was to live for four years. Aunt Mamie had saved supper for me, but the long eventful day, my first long trip and so far from home, overwhelmed me with homesickness. So I asked for my bedroom – where I cried myself to sleep. This I remember as one of the most tragic nights of my life.

The little grocery store was diagonally across the street from home – at Butte and Bremer streets. I was called next morning and sent to the store to sweep, cleanup and get things in order for the opening that day, at which time uncle Ed came in to get things ready for serving customers. I learned fast and soon adjusted to the change, largely because I was pleased to be able to send home one dollar each week for my mother, and about every other week I was able to send her two dollars. After working for several months and having learned to be of great service, I asked uncle Ed for an increase to two dollars a week which amount I could send home much better than the one dollar and a half. Of course, I had to keep a little of my salary for haircuts and a few clothes, but receiving room and board as part of my wages meant that my expenses were very small.

Early Influences

My teeth had never been cared for; whenever I had a toothache I just had them pulled. After I had worked for a year I wanted to have my teeth filled and to take better care of them. We had a dentist who was a good customer, so I asked him about doing the work for me. After telling him of my low financial ability, he candidly did the work for me, giving me time to pay a very small amount each week over a very long time.

During the second year, I was in need of more clothes and bought my first pants and coat, paying a small amount regularly over a long period..

I had been of such good help I was making eight dollars a week before my second year of work, and the third year, $10 per week, making it possible for me to send more and more home to my mother.

During my second year there, another one of my father's sisters, Aunt Stella Cook, whose husband was Prof. Arthur Cook of Wofford College in Spartanburg, South Carolina (he was a teacher of languages there), on a visit with Aunt Mamie, offered to take me back with her and give me a home and send me to school and then to college. Knowing the great needs of my mother, I stated my reason for not accepting their wonderful offer. I never informed my mother regarding the matter.

I had not been able to return home since I left four years ago. I decided to return and try for employment where I would be near my parents. I first found a job in Chatham with John R. Yeatts, who operated a big store near the railway station in Chatham, and worked there for a year at $10 per week and board. I occupied a small bedroom in the store building.

Chapter 2

Before Time

In the beginning was the word, and the word was with God, and the word was God. Bible

My notes;

From conversations later during my life, I am confident that while he was working in Chatham at the Yeatts' general store he had contact with his childhood school mate, Kate Reynolds. I do not know the details of their relationship. She did marry Bruce Edwards, and I heard mother speak of her having a daughter named Ethel and she having a daughter named Katie.

This short summary of four years living with his Uncle and Aunt and working in their store never mentions any social life with his Grand parents or cousins. Even though his Grandfather was a Methodist preacher, no mention of church or Sunday School attendance, and no weekend activities of fishing or time on the beach. A strange omission of any social contacts.

Evidently, to me, nothing of importance to him, but a lot of questions for me. For a boy in his early teens to have no curiosity or social life is beyond my comprehension. He was smart, a fast learner and had a pleasant personality with customers. Could that have been his entire life? My imagination could propose some of the experiences he may have had, but they would not be what actually happened in his life. So a blank time for anyone other than himself to know anything about.

Edgar Junior loved his father and understood the true reason for his addiction to whiskey and opium, but he was ashamed of his father's reputation in the community. His life mission was firmly set.

"Live a life so morally correct and so socially admired that he would atone through his own life and that of his future family for the reputation of his father." While he was working in Norfolk, he started signing his name E. P. and assumed the name Edwin Paul when required to reveal his full name.

Paul's Transcription Continues:

After working at the Yeatts store a year, Dr. Jones, a druggist and proprietor of Chatham Pharmacy, offered me a job to operate the soda fountain and gradually learn the drug business, which after serving for two years as an apprentice, I could go to the medical college in Richmond for the study of pharmacy for two years and earn a degree as a registered pharmacist. I had always wanted to be a medical doctor and saw in this plan an opportunity for me to reach for this career. I could work as a pharmacist and earn while attending medical school, thus providing the necessary finances. Then, too, the condition of my father had become such as to require a constant and dependable supply of drugs. This I was able to supply at cost through the drug store.

Dr. Jones gave me room and board in his home in South Chatham. I went to the store uptown early to clean up, sweep and open for business, later returning home for breakfast. It was on such trips that I would frequently meet a near neighbor, a Miss Ethel Whitehead, who was on her way to work in the store of her brothers, Whitehead and Yeatts. At first we only smiled and exchanged brief but pleasant greetings, as we had not formally met. Within a short time, I wrote and asked to take her to a night service at the Chatham Baptist Church. This was the beginning of a courtship that lasted for 50 years and 21 days, until the death of my wonderful wife and mother of six wonderful children.

My parents died in February and April 1908 (I was then 19 years of age). A guardian was appointed to settle my mother's estate, which consisted of the farm and a small amount of household furniture. My two years as a pharmacy apprentice was up in August. I informed our guardian about my plans to study pharmacy and my desire to enter the University College of medicine in Richmond in September, the beginning of the first semester. He informed me that it would take some time to wind up the estate, for me to borrow as much as $100 to pay the fees, for books and a month's room and board, and by that time he would send me my share of my mother's estate. Naturally, I had great difficulty in borrowing that much money, but finally persuaded Uncle Charles Shepard to let me have it, giving him a demand note for the amount payable with interest out of the funds from the estate. Ethel and I had been engaged for some time, but both agreed to defer our marriage for two years – until after my graduation.

I had a lot of trouble meeting the entrance requirements to the school of pharmacy on account of my very limited education – only a few years in the lower grades; but with great help from my last schoolteacher, Miss Blanche Haynes, the good recommendation of my employer, Dr. John M Jones, and a good record of progress made in practical experience, I was accepted. I went to Richmond in August, 1908 (I had just turned 20 on the previous June 12), found a board and rooming house, paid for one month, matriculated and bought the necessary books and supplies - all of which took most of the hundred dollars. I was accepted by and initiated into the college medical fraternity and settled down to study after long, hard and, at times, very discouraging circumstances. Before the month was up, I was informed by our guardian that after paying all the medical drug and funeral expenses for both my father and mother there would not be any funds to send me, that the land would have to be subdivided between the three children and that all of this would take about a year; that if I couldn't borrow enough for my first year of school I had better return to Chatham.

I discussed my situation with Dr. Rudd, the dean of the college, for his advice as to my getting a job and working for the first year. He advised against this: the first year was the most difficult and, with my very limited education it was most inadvisable. I returned to Chatham, but from no one could I obtain credit. This ended all of my plans, in sad disappointment.

This was not only a great disappointment but another crisis in my troubled life. It was, of course, also a great disappointment to Ethel. I was without a job, $100 in debt, and had no assets at all. In much heartache, doubts and fears, Ethel and I decided that both of us together could better solve our problems by getting married.

My notes;

Mother was 23 years old and had been dating George Stone for a few years. He was a family member of a prominent farming family east of Chatham and had graduated from VPI with an engineering degree. Their romantic interest was illustrated in the VPI 1907 or 1908 Annual with a picture of Mother and George who had chosen her as the "Sweetheart" of the company he was Captain of. Mother had a copy of the annual that she kept and that I saw years later. It had a tan swede leather cover. The page with the pictures of her and George showed him in his uniform facing the picture of Mother. Her picture was facing him and sort of surrounded as an oval resembling an opal ornament. Mother was nearly 40 when I was born and was always fat with a "bun" hair style, so that picture of her as a really beautiful young lady was one I treasured. After she was either engaged or married to Daddy, George asked why she had not married him. Her paraphrased answer was something like this: "You never asked and I was not getting any younger."

Paul's transcript continues.

If there ever was a marriage on love and faith, this was it. I got a friend to endorse a $50 note at the bank for money to buy necessary clothes, and to pay the preacher. So, on December 9, 1908 (I had just turned 20 years of age on the preceding June 12) we were married in Ethel's home in South Chatham, Virginia, Dr. T. Ryland Sanford performing the ceremony. Ethel was living with and keeping house for her mother, so we continued living there for several months. Dr. Jones wanted me back in the drugstore, where I worked for a while, but the salary was too small. With my additional responsibilities, I became local Manager of the Telephone Company and was, also, appointed Deputy Treasurer to collect taxes in Chatham District. With both jobs, we rented a small house uptown with two rooms and set up house keeping. We were happy to be out on our own. For the first three years I had a hard time – without education or special qualifications it was difficult to obtain work with sufficient dependable income. In the third year our first of six children was born, Sally Hunt, named for her Grandmother Whitehead.

Before Time

Next came Louisa Anderson, named for her Grandmother Crider. About this time a vacancy occurred in the Chatham savings bank and Ethel's brother Hurt recommended me for the job – but it was given to Harry Pritchett. Soon after this, Planters Savings Bank offered me a job as Assistant Cashier. Hurt, who was also a partner in Chatham's largest mercantile business, offered me a working partnership in that business. After considering the two offers, Ethel and I decided on the bank position, which I accepted, and went to work at $50 per month in 1912.

I made great progress and became efficient in all work, both as teller and bookkeeper of all the books, in individual accounts and the general ledger. We then rented a small house in West Chatham and soon made progress in our needs and living standard. I was anxious to buy a small house or vacant lot and build. One Sunday we were visiting friends who owned a farm just south of Chatham. He suggested our buying a lot on his farm and build a home there, as he would be pleased to have us as neighbors. With this in mind, we bought a lot of 3 acres – one acre wide on Route 29 on the Danville Road and running back three acres. The price was $125. We made a contract for building a small home with an understanding with the firm of Whitehead and Yates to sell me the lumber and building materials on a long-time basis, to be paid by me in monthly installments. Good progress was made, and soon the kitchen was finished. We then moved into the one room until the house was finally completed. For some reason the sellers of the materials thought the cost was too high and they wanted me to sell and pay up. I found a purchaser and sold the house, and we moved out before it was finished. This is the house in South Chatham – now known as "Woodlawn" – which was the *first one to be built out there and is now owned by Ms. Asa Viccellio.*

This failure in home ownership continued Daddy's life in the shadow of the Whitehead family.

Paul's note that he sent with a copy of the above manuscript:

I only wish that I could have known him – and he me – don't you wish the same?

I did not have much contact with my daddy until late in his life. He was mostly a visitor in our home. Saved for financial support, discipline and vacations. All of which he generously provided. He seldom talked about his parents or his life experiences.

A man with a burden of hard-earned experiences that were then a large part of who he was as a psychological person. Until his marriage and first child, only a few people outside his work environment were mildly affected by associating with him. A man with such little formal education as to be none. Equivalent to four grades in a one-teacher, two-room log house. No professional credentials to show a potential employer.

Now a family man with financial responsibility and his double burden of the shameful reputation of his father and the inferior, by marriage, member of an aristocratic family. Not much he could do except to accept his status and strive to demonstrate his worthiness. A good job reputation with recommendations by his employers, but all with journeyman responsibilities. A long and dreary path ahead for him and his family.

The Whiteheads, also, were degraded by having one of their own being just a clerk and journeyman. Their status as educated, independent business owners, high social class and politically and financially powerful was at risk. They knew Daddy was of good moral character, personally appealing and mentally capable. A solution to the blemish on their influence and reputation was to take him into their business as a partner or manager-level member. Two options were offered. General store partner, where Daddy had many years of experience, or bank Assistant Cashier. With Mother's agreement, he chose the job in the bank.

Looking back from many past years, the job at the bank was his only secure choice. From his previous retail store experiences and his desire to show his independent capability, store management differences would have likely caused irreparable conflicts. The Cashier job in the bank was a fresh start, a desire to learn and to perform at a high level. His driving attempt to never allow his feeling of inferiority to show, and his natural intelligence and friendly personality ensured his success. Nothing ever deprived him of his journey and goal.

His life mission was firmly set. "Live a life so morally correct and so socially admired that he would atone through his own life and that of his future family for the reputation of his father." While he was working in Norfolk, he started signing his name E. P. and assumed the name Edwin Paul when required to reveal his full name.

I have found that who a person is and becomes is the total of his/her experiences, each as an historical event and attached emotions, attitudes, opinions for each event. Also, the historical event is not changeable by the person, but, through the thinking process of comparisons, a person compares new similar experiences with older ones and can change the older emotional ones to be more rational in light of more relevant information. Thus, two ways that we continually evolve as who we are as a person are through new experiences and, if we desire, changing our remembered emotional attachments to more rational and desirable ones.

I am sure that Daddy never knew or questioned his embedded memories that drove him. They were as originally experienced and rode him throughout his life. Success in all that he did and who he appeared to be, and shining examples of his family as successful in all that they did. Physical appearance and honest, truthful, moral and religious character.

Not an easy life to live, and more so to be married into a much higher social, political and financial aristocratic family. Daddy wrote of his hard life and several crushing disappointments, but he did not mention his feeling of inferiority among Mother's family.

An opportunity for home ownership came, but with strings attached. Mother's inheritance came from her brother Hurt, the executor of her father's will. A two-third acre lot on the edge of Uncle Hurt's farm was chosen for her, and $1,500.00 in cash. One narrow edge of the rectangular lot fronted on an unimproved farm road, Viccellio Street, about 150 yards from Main Street and had only two unimproved houses for Uncle Hurt's black farm tenants. The other narrow edge joined the Main Street Jones lot, and the other long side joined Uncle Walter's Main Street lot. A very undesirable location and hidden from view from Main Street. No appeal. No questions allowed.

This inheritance was an opportunity for home ownership in Mother's name, and, with Daddy's agreement, she took it. A Cape Cod one-and-a-half story house was built, and Mother, Daddy, Sallie and Lou moved in.

Daddy was working in Planter's Bank where Uncle Hurt was President and Chairman of the Board of Directors. Daddy owed a lot to Uncle Hurt for the job given to him, and he was paying a lot in excellent work and in hidden humiliation of living on a dirt road among black farm tenants. He made the most of his situation, and demanded a lot from his oldest child, Sallie, and only a little less from Lou. A show of perfection to prevent any indication of a past and forgotten humiliating reputation of his father. Even Daddy was not consciously aware of this influence on his life. Hidden so deeply in his memory he did not know it had become a part of who he psychologically was.

Another girl baby, Ethel, was born 11/15/1917. She was infected with erysipelas and died less than three months later. Daddy bought a lot in the Chatham Town cemetery and buried her there. Another loss with another sad memory.

World war in Europe started, and the United States joined the conflict. County Draft Boards were established when there were not enough volunteers, and all men under the age of 40 were classified according to eligibility for military duty. Because of his family responsibility, Daddy was less likely to be among the early draftees. Still, as the war continued, that threat was ever present in Mother's and Daddy's life. Finally the war ended, and in 1920 another baby girl, Katie, was born. Daddy's "1920 model" and his obvious favorite.

Times were good except where he and his family were living. Uncle Walter agreed to sell Mother an acre lot from his Main-Street-fronting lot and let her family live in the second floor of his house while her house was being moved up the hill from her lot in the bottoms. Generosity and sibling love expressed in material value.

The method used to move large houses and other buildings was to jack them up high enough to put temporary long sill timbers underneath and then place large, straight logs crosswise to the sills and direction of movement as rolling supports. Power for pulling was by teams of horses and mules. As movement progressed, logs passed over at the back were brought to the front to be used as a roller again. A slow and careful process; especially so over soft or wet ground. What started as a projected six- month project ran into unprecedented rain and, as winter came, snow and ice.

Mother and Daddy never talked much about their extended stay in Uncle Walter's second floor. Unpredicted things did happen. At least one major one: Paul, Junior was born there. It was a hard birth. Both Mother and baby Paul suffered. In a final resolve, Dr. Parish broke one of Paul's arms and placed it to allow his birth. Saved both Mother's and Paul's life. An unrealistic but real resentment of Paul, Jr. that Daddy carried hidden and unexpressed in words, but real enough in deed.

Paul, Jr. survived with his little arm in a cast. Painful, restrictive and cumbersome for him and his caregivers. A hindrance to daily sanitation and a severe limitation to playing, nursing and "normal" baby life. This encumbered daily life gradually became more normal physically and emotionally until Daddy's expectations of his first son and namesake started demanding more.

More than a year in Uncle Walter's second floor until the house was ready for occupancy. I never heard of any cross words or expressions of stress, and I only experienced friendship and family love. Being on two levels and separate entrances restricted much interaction.

Sunday January 6, 1924, Christian Epiphany, was the coldest day of that winter as I was told by my mother and older sisters. At high noon in our house at what is now 343 South Main Street in Chatham after the water pipes were thawed and Dr. Parrish and a helper lady arrived, a 12-pound baby boy arrived from a 5'2" 212-pound mother --- ME!! Being the last of 5 children in my family and the last of about 30 neighbor maternal first cousins in the very small town of Chatham, I was much loved and cared for (except by my older brother, Paul, until we were mature adults). Thus began my continuing process of developing physically and mentally as a human person.

Physically, I was fat which was soon lost, and I developed eczema causing severe skin rash and pain. Wet and messy diapers made the pain worse. Remedies of several kinds of salves were tried without much relief. Another treatment tried was bathing me in buttermilk. I think this may have helped a little but left me smelling like sour milk. After what must have seemed like an eternity to my mother and two older sisters, the eczema cleared, and my physical development continued normally.

My oldest sister, Sallie, was 13 when I was born, and my next oldest sister, Lou, was 11. My first learning came from them and my mother. As a baby my responses to situations I was exposed to were mainly pre-set reflexes to various kinds of stimuli. Even during this period of infancy, like other babies, I was learning to recognize sensory stimuli, objects and people. I did not know how to express my own feelings about or to name or understand what or who these sensory stimuli, objects and people were, but I was learning what was pleasing and what was not. The only expressions in response were laughing or crying.

An independent, breathing, marvelous, self-building physical and physiological human and starting the process of becoming a psychological person. From even before that eventful day my physiological system was building my physical and physiological structure and function from my genetic instructions. I continued growing according to my genetic design, and started using my sensory stimuli to develop my psychological mind.

Always changing. Never the same. Adjusting by comparing my physical status to my genetic design and my psychological status to my past sensory experiences. Each day a challenge and an opportunity. My psychological person started with the social life I was born into. A Southern Baptist racist. No choice on my part. My parents, older siblings, maternal uncles and aunts and 30 maternal first cousins all living in the very small town of Chatham, VA. All telling me by living the life that I should live. Nothing else to compare it with, and even if I had and wanted to change, I would have nothing to change to.

I developed the skin disease, eczema. A treatment given to me was daily bathing in buttermilk. It or my natural immune system finally cured the disease and gave me a normal skin and "normal" baby odor instead of that of sour milk. Later, my older sisters said that I generally was a happy baby and "into everything." I was my mother's "baby" for the rest of her life.

Before Time

Daddy worked, and his family grew and developed according to his psychological person. Sallie, the oldest, and Paul, the first son, had his highest expectations and received his expressed (emotional and verbal) severe disappointments. .

Sallie was the flagship of Daddy's family. One who was exposed to the local world as Paul Crider's daughter. She was expected to do nothing that did not represent superior in all aspects. A burden too great for a child to understand or to bear. She had above average intelligence, but was kept from starting school when she was old enough so that she could go with her younger sister, Lou. Started out well and according to plan, but soon came apart. Sallie skipped a grade into second grade and left Lou behind. Lou did not care, and Sallie made the promotion seem like a natural transition. By then, Daddy took her recognition of superior ability to be within his "normal" expectation. Nothing more. Nothing less. The way things were supposed to be. No accolades for Sallie from Daddy, but his lack of praise a disappointment for Sallie. What would she have to do to get Daddy's approval? Probably not her first lost effort, but the first I know about.

Sallie continued on in-home and out-of-home pre-teen years. House-keeping and childcare, staying away from negro neighbor children, excelling in piano lessons from Mrs. Bolanz and in both appearance and performance in her graduation concert. The last was a beginning of an expression of independence by Sallie. She did not touch the keyboard of a piano again until many years later as pianist in her church. Daddy demanded too much from his oldest child. Her life was hers, and the part that pleased Daddy just naturally happened as part of what she wanted to do and not because of his discipline. Good grades in school came naturally for her, and she dressed and conducted herself to be attractive to others. A fun-loving and happy personality. Not a lot for Daddy to complain about.

Sallie flirted with high-school boys, but nothing serious enough for Daddy to be concerned about.

Chapter 3

Contrast of Brothers

Brothers for a lifetime: through thick and thin.

I was the last of six children born to my mother and father. One died as an infant, so there were five siblings living in our house when I was born. Three sisters and two brothers. Paul was chronologically two years older than I, but emotionally and psychologically he was already a mature adult compared to me. That difference remained throughout our child and adolescent life. Our two oldest sisters had very little influence on our developing lives except for early child care. My sister Katie was two years older than Paul and four years older than I. She usually did not share the authoritarian subjugation from Paul that I did, and was a refuge for me from some of it.

Sallie was often given responsibility for my care. At her age, she was not consistently attentive and alternated from playful sister to distracted inattention, especially as she developed into her mid teens. Boys at her school and those attending the local boarding school, Hargrave Military Academy, were more on her mind than looking after me. When I started getting mobility by crawling, my inquisitive character started being expressed. Everything was new, exciting and had to be explored and examined. I some how climbed on a chest of drawers and ate laxative gum. I learned how to escape the expanding gate across our front porch entry and was, after much frantic calling and searching, located across the street in the porch swing of my Aunt Elizabeth. I was later told of these events repeatably until I feel I remember them. Later, I do actually remember some of the happenings in my first five years that we lived in Chatham.

Each pair of my grandparents had children, some with as many as ten that lived to adulthood. With sparse population in the early and late 1800s and very little travel outside the immediate locality, marriages mostly were between neighbors. Thus, when I was born, my parents were kin by either blood or marriage to several families in the county. In the small town of Chatham I was a family member to most residents in Chatham and to many families in the Five Points area of the county. Because my early life was most influenced by my mother, my siblings and my mother's siblings and their families all of whom lived in or near Chatham, they had the most early influence on my development.

Being the youngest of my 30 neighbor cousins often left me behind in their play. They did not want me as a responsibility to interfere with their more "mature" activities. One that I did fit in well with was the tire-rolling play. I could sit in the upright tire with arms and legs holding the inside rim while it was shoved upright to roll down hill in Uncle Hurt's front yard. Someone was supposed to catch the tire with me at the bottom of the hill before it lost speed and turned over. Sometimes they did, sometimes they didn't and sometimes I hit a tree. I don't think I was ever hurt much, and at least I was part of the older children's play!

I also watched Paul and Katie take part in play with our cousins that I was too young to participate. After their going to a circus in Danville, Uncle Hurt's children reenacted some of the acts they saw. Anna, the older girl would swing on a rope tied to a rafter in their stable and make daring moves and fall into the hay. Attempts to juggle balls was another, and they told of the strange animals and clown acts. One memorable occasion was a magician-type act that Paul and a couple of cousins put on in Uncle Hurt's attic. Mind reading was exhibited one evening with my parents and Uncle Hurt and Aunt Elizabeth also attending and giving much applause and laughter.

Uncle Hurt was the major owner of Planters Bank and also owned a wholesale store in Chatham. Daily he walked to work and back. When Paul and I were in our yard, he would pick each up and in turn give us a breath-taking "bear hug" and some candy or other treat from his store.

Uncle Walter lived next door to us and had two sons about the same age as Sallie and Lou. On some summer evenings a few of us cousins would play the game of "Mother May I", tag and hide and seek in his front yard and long concrete walk. When I was instructed to "take three large steps forward", I would often forget to ask, "Mother May I" and get penalized to start over.

Another Uncle who gave special attention to Paul and me was Uncle Doug. He owned a livery stable in Chatham, but he lived about a mile south of the town limits. He rode a horse by our house on his way to work and back. He and his wife, Aunt Minnie, did not have children. He wore western-style boots, clothes and hat, and he had a braided leather whip. When Paul and I were in our yard when he passed, he would call to us and give us very gentle "growing lashes" with his whip. Sometimes he would lift me into the saddle and Paul holding on behind and give us a short ride. On one occasion he gave us a ride to a pond behind our house and had his horse swim across the pond with us on the horse with him.

When I was about four, I started having wheezing and breathing attacks. I don't think any effective treatment was known. I was just required to rest until the spell was past.

The upright piano that Sallie used to practice her lessons could also be played "normally" as she did or with a self-playing roller.

On one occasion I remember Daddy pretended he was playing while using the self-playing feature. A wide paper roll with small holes that matched where keys were actually played the piece, but Daddy put on the acting show. One of the few times I remember he was in a playful mood with us children.

We also got a Victrola record player with hand-winder handle and spring drive and some needles and Bakelite records. Sallie and Lou used this some to keep up with modern songs.

Both of these were in our parlor which was usually reserved for non-family visitors and special occasions. Because it had a fireplace with a chimney, It was our place for Christmas holidays. We had a tree with decorations, and colorful stockings hanging on the mantel. The chimney was a special mail service directly to Santa Claus at the North Poll. Each of us would write or, in my case, have someone who could write, a wish list on a small piece of paper. Then carefully hold it above the flames near the "throat" of the fireplace and let the fast-rising hot air take it up and out the top of the chimney to a swift ride directly to Santa and his elves. Magic to us smallest children.

Daddy was working at Planters Bank in Chatham during those years, and in 1928 he changed jobs to the Commercial Bank in Danville. Daddy rode the bus 18 miles to work and back. Rowland Reynolds, a man Daddy knew from near Five Points was the driver. During that commuting Daddy bought a new Model T Ford in Danville and, because no driving license was required, he drove it home. He had never driven a car before and only had driving instructions from the car salesman before driving it home. He and all of us were very excited about the car and wanted to go for a ride. We got in, and Daddy drove up Main Street and around the circle at the north end of town and back home. While going around the circle we all thought we would be thrown out or the car would turn over because Daddy did not slow down.

I guess I was about 3 or 4 and my sister Lou was about 14 when she won a subscription sales contest by the *Danville Register* newspaper . Her prize was a pony and cart. He had brown and white markings and she named him "Dandy." I was "too young" to join Lou, Katie, Paul and cousin Katie Doug in a ride that ended in a runaway down Cherrystone Creek hill south of town, overturn and scrapes, bruises and minor cuts for the passengers. The injured came straggling home or given a ride by passers-by. I don't remember the incident, but it was told so vividly and often that I feel I had experienced it. Youth had it's advantage then. The incident did not have a chance for a repeat. Dandy and his cart were soon sold, and Lou exchanged them for "money in the bank."

Paul suffered from emotional stress of Daddy's impossible expectations and lack of appreciation of his superior performances. Never enough or good enough to please him. None of us understood Daddy's emotional feeling of disappointment in everything that Paul and Sallie did and the life they lived. I'm sure that Daddy was not cognitively aware that the burden of shame of his father's reputation ruled his life and through him the lives of his family. But it did, and it became a burden for his family too.

Contrast of Brothers

I only have a few memories of Paul during my first four or five years. I think the first was when he was about six When Dr. Parrish came and went into our room with Paul and Mother, and I was told to stay out doors. After the doctor left, I came back in and asked Paul what the doctor did. He said that he had operated on his penis and that it had hurt and was still hurting. Paul walked real slow and careful for about a week. Dr, Parrish came back to check on Paul and said that he was healing and would no longer need to bandage and put medicine on the wound. Paul said that his penis still hurt when it rubbed against his under pants.

I was always too young to go do things with my brother and sister when they went farther than Uncle Hurt's or Uncle Walter's yards, and a lot of times I was mostly an observer.

Paul was the dare devil in our family and would show his risk-taking often. One way was climbing trees. One tree, a " Stink-weed" (Catalpa) , grew against the low edge of our garage roof. Paul would climb onto the roof and slide down the tree. Another was an "umbrella" tree in our back yard. Paul would climb up and out on one of the springy limbs and play riding a horse. The perch was not secure enough for the bouncing, and Paul fell several feet to land on his stomach. His observer, Sallie, saw Paul struggling for breath and pushed on his chest repeatedly until he started breathing on his own.

Daddy's commuting did not last long until we moved to a rented apartment on Sutherlin Ave. in Danville. I think that there were no professional movers, but Uncle Doug's workers used his cattle truck to move our things. At that time there were overhead wooden trusses supporting the bridge across Cherrystone Creek just south of Chatham, and Mother's bedroom wardrobe top facade was too high and was broken off. It wasn't missed until the furniture was unloaded, and it was never found. Mother was upset for a long time about loosing that decoration.

Sutherlin Avenue was a long one-block residential street between South Main Street and Green Street. Moving our furniture into the upstairs apartment was not an easy job, not even for experienced movers. The stairs from the front porch were narrow and steep. The porch had several steps to the front walk and there were banisters around it. Finally, everything was moved in except the upright piano which was not only very heavy; it also was to large to fit in the stair well. It was an amateur engineering challenge, and the plan also required approval from Mrs. Lion who lived on the first floor and was the landlady. Finally, a spectator event when an upstairs window was removed, ropes and pulley from a roof-top beam were used to gradually hoist the piano up the outside of the house and pulled in through the vacant window frame. I don't know if there was any applause, but I think there was a sigh of relief from my Mother and probably from the workers and some of the spectators too.

Thus we started our residence knowing no one, but being known or being known of by most of the residents on our new street.

Even though we had moved only a distance of about 18 miles, our lifetime residence and neighbors were gone, and we, were in a strange and unknown place. Sallie was at Harrisonburg State Teachers College, and Lou was living with us as a day student at Averett College in Danville. Daddy had taken Paul to enroll in the first grade at the elementary school on Holbrook Boulevard, the next street parallel to ours, and Katie was attending another school. After it was time for Paul to come home from school, Mother began to worry about him. She took me with her to look for him. He was sitting on the curb at the corner of Holbrook and Green Streets not knowing which way to go. He seemed more ashamed than glad to see us, but Mother and I were glad to see him.

After we had sort of begun to settle into our new place, I was enrolled in Peter Pan Kindergarten. I was given transportation by the kindergarten, and I have some recollection of coloring and pasting. I did not attend long before I was diagnosed with tonsillitis. My first cousin, Dr. Howell Watson, was the surgeon. He was 24 years older than I and one of my oldest maternal cousins. I would never forget fighting the ether-administering mask and vomiting green slime after the operation. I think I remained in the Memorial Hospital in Danville for a day before coming home. That ended my kindergarten experience.

I tagged along as Katie and Paul made friends on our street and played with them. I was a "student" in some of Katie's play classes, and I watched some of their card games of very limited strip poker. Another neighbor who lived on Green Street at the end of Sutherlin had a monkey and a parrot. Green Street Park joined their back yard. They had made a bird trap consisting of a box with the open side down and supported on one edge by a short stick with a long string attached. They had poured a thin line of bird feed from several feet from the box to a small pile underneath. Holding the string in their open window and waiting until a bird was eating under the box and then pulling the stick allowed the box to drop and sometimes catch a bird. I don't know what was done with the birds they caught.

On the Main Street end of Sutherlin there was a fire station and

The Sutherlin Museum and Library. We would visit the Museum and were very interested in looking at the paired pictures through a stereoscope card holder. The ones that were most interesting were of the World War. We also liked to look at the fire engines and talk to the firemen at the fire station.

A neighbor boy and I bought a box of matches from a small convenience store on Green Street and were learning to strike them in the alley behind our house. A very interesting and exciting experience to see the end of the match stick suddenly burst into flame and sort of sizzle. I must have been frightened by one of the igniting matches and dropped it in some dead leaves alongside the picket fence that was attached to the side our house. The effort of both of us to put the resulting fire out seemed to make the flames bigger. My friend went home, and I hid in the alley some distance from the fire. I watched as the flames grew larger. Then the fire truck came from our fire station with flashing lights and wailing sirens, and the firemen soon had the fire out. Lots of neighbors looked on. I went on up the alley and out onto the Sutherlin walk and walked home.

I evidently had not learned how to lie effectively because my efforts to portray innocence failed. When Daddy came home, he was told what I had done and took charge of my punishment. I had accumulated a bank saving account which would be used to pay for damages caused by the fire. I also received physical punishment to improve my memory of the incident so I would not repeat doing such a bad thing. Daddy had a pair of razor straps, one leather and one canvas, that he used to sharpen his straight razor. He demonstrated another very handy use across my

45

bare behind while verbally giving me further direction, warnings and guidance. His efforts were effective as my memory is still fresh, and I have been extremely careful with matches.

During the summer while there was no school, the children on our street would play together at various games and would visit different yards, homes, the museum and the park from one end of Sutherlin to the other. My mother knew we were somewhere on the street and often did not hear her call. She solved that by blowing a police whistle from the upstairs balcony. If we did not hear the whistle, other children who did passed the word along.

One day Lou took Katie, Paul and me to a movie. It was one that Lou really wanted to see, "Uncle Tom's Cabin." We rode the street car down town, and started watching what to me became a very real and scary experience. The part when Simon Legree with his whip and dogs were chasing his run-away slaves north to the river they were trying to cross to freedom and Little Eva fell through the ice, I totally broke down with loud crying. Other people in the theater started complaining so much that Lou had to take me outside. She was so disappointed and upset with me she complained for about a week.

Sometimes in a wide age group we just walked along from one yard to another talking and looking. On one time of meandering, one of the older boys told a really pretty girl about my age,Jean Yarborough, "I'll show you mine if you will show me yours." She said , "Alright."

He opened his pants and showed his penis, and she then raised her dress and pulled her panties down. I looked , but I did not see anything but just skin. Later I asked Paul if he saw anything, and he said he did. I don't know if he really did though. That Jean was the mascot of Lou's class at Averett College, and Lou told me that she really liked me.

After about a year living on Sutherlin Avenue, we moved to a larger side-by-side two-story brick duplex on West Main Street. It was across the street from the hospital nurse's dormitory and on the corner with West End Avenue. Across that street was a hospital for Negroes.

Sallie had graduated from Chatham High School and went to Harrisonburg State Teachers College in Harrisonburg, VA. Majored in elementary education, and after two years she received a teaching certificate.

Uncle Fletcher Watson was the County School Superintendent and approved Sallie's application to teach first grade at Schoolfield Elementary School located in the suburbs of Danville. She came home to live with us on West Main St. Lou was still enrolled at Averett College, and they together were friends with much older retired Major John Hurt who was living in the Lealand Hotel. He enjoyed their company during long rides in his convertible Chevrolet and was especially attracted to Lou who was 17. Her being underage for marriage without her parent's consent, he asked Daddy for his consent. I think Lou was willing, but Daddy said, "No." When Lou finished the two years of Junior College offered at Averett, she then went to Norfolk to train as a nurse in a hospital there.

Our next-door neighbor who shared the duplex with us had a son, Nelson Benton, about Paul's age. We played together some, and Paul and Katie made other friends too. I followed along. One of Paul's friends was an Anderson boy whose family was very rich. He had a pony and cart and a grazing lot and stable in their back yard. They had a chauffeur-driven big black limousine and took Paul on some rides in it. I was watching when dead grass in their grazing lot was being burned. I fell down in some smoldering grass as I was running from the flames and got a bad burn on one leg. Salve and time helped it heal. Mrs. Anderson invited Katie, Paul and me to lunch. It was very formal for us, and I think we behaved very well. She had a servant who brought food and carried away used dishes when she was given a ring from a bell operated by Mrs. Anderson's foot pedal. I did not like the spinach that was served, and she encouraged me to eat it.

I started first grade at an elementary school on Grove Street about 4 or 5 blocks from our house. That whole year continues as a blur. There was a really cute girl in my class who lived in an apartment along our route and walked to school with us.

Lou came home to get married in April, 1931 to a man she had met in Norfolk, Robert Morgan. I don't remember attending the wedding, but I do remember the wedding party leaving. Lou, Robert and his two sisters drove away with a lot of waving hands and good wishes.

Sallie dated several boyfriends, and she lived an independent life on her income. Lots of shoes and dresses. Sometimes she helped me with my first-grade homework, but mostly we did not see each other except at meal times. Daddy was not happy with her lifestyle, but she did not conform to his comments.

Daddy's work as head Cashier at the Commercial Bank went well except for an incident that cast doubt on his honesty and trust. Banks in Danville did daily business with each other by transferring checks and check payments to the bank of origin. A young man, known as a "Runner", was used to pick up and deliver these transfers. One of these transfers from Daddy was not received by the intended bank! The runner said that he was not given the missing package by Daddy. Emotional devastation for Daddy, but he confronted the challenge by hiring a secret detective who searched the runner's room and found the contents of the missing package in one of the runner's socks. Relief for Daddy.

In 1931 The Great Depression had a personal effect on us when the Commercial Bank became bankrupt. Daddy was chosen by the bankrupt court judge to close all accounts in a fair way for all depositors and debtors. This gave Daddy a temporary job and an office. As mortgage payments came in or assets (mostly farms) were sold, Daddy would distribute proportionate payments to account holders. I remember going to his office with my savings book and being paid about half of the amount in my book.

The severe financial depression caused a lot of emotional depression too. It also offered challenges of survival that tested resourcefulness. To reduce living expenses, Daddy needed money to buy his ancestral farm from his two sisters so we could live there. The farm had no financial value as mortgage security, but Mother's Chatham property could be used as collateral for a loan. They traded property leaving Daddy owning the house in Chatham and Mother owning the 90-acre farm. Daddy later bought Aunt Mary's 60 acre farm that had also been part of his mother's farm.

A few Sundays Daddy would drive us to Tomahawk to visit his sister, Aunt Nancy Gatewood, and her family who lived on the farm where he was born. We had a good time playing on the farm and in thes table hay loft with her children.

Many years later Louise, the oldest child of Aunt Nancy, told me that Daddy had paid her way in college to get a teaching certificate. It probably happened on one of our visits, and was only one of his many "silent" philanthropic gifts that I only found out about after Daddy had died.

The summer after I finished first grade, Aunt Nancy's family moved to Norfolk where her husband, Uncle Walter, got a job in the Norfolk Navy Yard. Mother did not drive, so Sallie would drive us to the farm where all of us would clean the house to get it ready for us to move into. The house was of wood-frame construction two- stories high with a small front porch. It had a rusty standing-seam metal A-frame roof sloping toward the front across two bedrooms on the second floor. The front door on the left side of the porch opened into a hall and stairway. The hall had doors to the living room on the right and to the side back porch at the back. The dining room was at the back of the living room and behind that was a shed-roof kitchen that had doors outside at the back, to a large pantry and to the side shed-roof porch. There was a rock chimney between the living and dining rooms and extended up between two of the bedrooms. There was another rock chimney outside the back wall of the kitchen. The inside walls and ceilings were finished with 4-inch-wide beaded lap-sided boards with narrow cracks between them. There was no plumbing or electric wiring. There was painted wood flooring in all the rooms and wood steps at the entrances. Aunt Nancy had left the house fairly clean, but Mother wanted it cleaner, and we did some interior painting. Because there were bedbugs, Mother would light "sulfur candles" and close all doors and windows before we left.

Chapter 4

A Century Backward

Resourcefulness tested

By summer's end we had moved to the farm that Daddy named "Windcrest." I was 7 when I started second grade at Climax High & Elementary School in 1931. Daddy still had his job in Danville and drove to work and back daily. Transition and adjustment to life-changing environment and living conditions were awesome! Mother had found her Happy Place! Soon I think we three children found ours too. Sallie stayed in Danville and continued teaching and came home during the summers. Daddy hired a man about 20 years old, Clyde Adkins, to work on the farm and around the house. He was newly married to Maisie Barber who was about 15. They lived in the three-room log cabin that Daddy had lived in as a child. It had a separate driveway and was farther off the public road and behind our house.

Our nearest neighbor was the Jessie Bowen family who lived across the "big road", along a foot path, across a creek, up a steep hill and on to their house. It was about a half-mile from our house. The farm road from their house went to the big road near Greenpond Baptist Church about a mile from our house and a much longer walk for them than to their mail box which they put next to ours. Either Mr. Bowen or his wife, Minnie, came to their mail box daily and would often visit with Mother. They had three children about the ages of us, Raleigh, Missouri and Larry. They also had three older girls, Blanche, Ruby and Ethel. They were sharecroppers on a farm owned by Mr. Bowen's father, Billy, who also owned a general store at Climax. There also were two other families living in houses on their farm, John Adkins and his wife Mary, who was

Mr. Bowen's sister, and their two boys, Malcolm and Jack, who were Paul's and my age and the other "family" was Faitwash Linthicum and his two sisters. The Linthicums lived in a small house between our house and the Bowens, and the Adkins live beyond the Bowens. The Bowen children did not go to school because they did not have nice clothes and shoes and could not afford to buy books and supplies. I think that was the situation of some of the other white sharecropper families near us. I did not know any of the black families.

We did not see the Bowen children much during the school year, but during the summer we often played together either at their house or ours. Raleigh being older taught Paul and me how to make a slingshot from a forked limb, two strips from an old worn-out inner tube, a piece from the tongue of an old shoe and some string. Raleigh was a good shot, and once after whistling to stop a running rabbit, he hit it in the head with a small rock. He then ran to grab the stunned rabbit and finish killing it by knocking it behind it's head with a stick and bleeding it by cutting it's throat. Raleigh also taught us how to recognize and find rabbit paths and where and how to set box traps to catch them. Clyde helped us make a couple of traps which we set next to a rabbit path and checked daily. When I caught one, I would put the open end of a burlap bag tightly around the trap-door-end of the trap, open the door and tap on the trap to scare the rabbit into the bag and quickly close the bag with the rabbit inside. I would re-bait the trap with a piece of onion or apple and reset it before taking my exciting catch home.

Clyde showed me how to kill and "dress" my catch. If we were planning to cook and eat it, I would skin and clean the entrails out and cut

53

the head and feet off. If I planned to sell it at Walker's Store for a 10 cent wood due bill, I would just slit the rabbit down the center of it's belly and clean the entrails out. Mr. Walker bought produce from local farmers by paying in wood shape and size "coins" printed with, "Good only at Walkers Store for (amount) ". The amount depended on the value of the merchandise and size of the coin. I did not catch many that we did not eat.

Daddy bought a horse for Clyde to use on the farm and in the garden. He was tall, red, raw-boned and had a sort of independent attitude. Once when he had escaped the stable lot into our yard, he bared his teeth and charged toward Mother who was trying to help get him back into the lot. She just barely got out of his way. Clyde handled him alright, but Paul could only get a bridle on him when he was closed in a stall. I did not try.

Uncle Walter Gatewood had left some harness and farming implements, but all the out buildings and fences were in bad condition. Clyde cut some trees and hauled the logs on the wagon to Cousin Otey's mill to be sawed into lumber, and he worked on repairing the barb-wire fences. He also did the heavy outside work around the house. The outside "privy" was a one-hole dilapidated structure a little distance away in back of the house. Replacing that with a new two-hole one was the first of Clyde's building projects.

The lives of us three children were suddenly thrust back a century or more with the conditions we found at Windcrest. A big contrast from our lives in Chatham and Danville. Without electric service, we were left with very primitive conditions inside our house. No electric lights or cook

54

stoves; no central heat; no running water; no bath room; etc. To compensate for the lack of our previously assumed "necessities" required a lot of physical work from all of us, and it also required cooperation with each performing his/her assigned tasks. Mother assigned the chore tasks to each of us, and she followed up with enforcement. Katie had house keeping work, and Paul and I did outdoor jobs. We brought water in buckets along a path up a long hill from the spring. I had to stop and rest a time or two, and sometimes my bucket was not as near full as Mother said it should be. Our house was heated by a wood-burning heater in each room, and our food was cooked and water heated on a kitchen range. Clyde cut the trees and chopped and split them into stove sizes. Paul and I brought it in and kept the wood box in each room full. The heater in each bedroom was a thin sheet metal vertical oval cylinder with a swivel lid on top where wood was put in, a screw-stemmed circle of flat metal to regulate the air draft of a hole near the bottom in front and a flue opening and pipe in the top back to the chimney. They would heat rapidly and often get red hot. Our dining room had a large brown-enamel rectangular cage surrounding a cast iron fire box. It would burn wood or coal and, once warm would continue to stay warm much longer than the bedroom "tin heaters." There was a "Franklin" stove in the living room. It was a cast iron, open-front stove with a grate for wood or coal and a flue pipe to the chimney in back. It looked like a fire place sitting in the room, and had two removable cast iron front covers that were used to control the air draft. In addition to Uncle Doug's livery stable of farm-animals, he sold and delivered coal and wood. Feeding these stoves during the winter was a hard job for Paul and me, especially the upstairs ones. During the spring and summer this job was replaced with garden and yard work.

Cousin Otha Hudson drove the school bus that went by our house to the end of his route at the mill, turned around and picked us up on his way back toward the Climax Elementary and High School. Having this advance warning gave us time to meet the bus without having to wait at the main road very long. At first, Cousin Otha said that his route did not include our side road and would require us to walk a half mile to catch the bus. Mother agreed to pay him to come as far as our house. When Mother mentioned this to her sister, Aunt Katie Watson, it was not long before the bus route had been extended past our house to the mill by her husband, Uncle Fletcher, who was Superintendent of County schools.

Riding a bus to school was a new experience for us, and being new pupils at a strange school was confusing too. There were four buildings in a row with a large open field in front to the main road. two two-story tall wooden buildings; one for the four high school grades and one for grades 2 through 7. There was a one-story brick building for an auditorium/gym, first grade and agriculture and one one-story wooden residential-type house for the caretaker. The caretaker's house had one room with a separate entrance that was for home economics.

My second grade was on the first floor front. There were four concrete steps outside that had a landing at the top. The front door opened into a hall with a long stair way to the second floor where there were four classrooms. The downstairs hall opened into two classrooms on each side. Each classroom had a long cast iron boxwood heater and a closet for wood. After school each day the caretaker would charge each heater with paper, kindling and wood ready for the next day. My classroom had two-child benches and desks. The desk top had an ink well and a pencil groove in front of each pupil. My teacher was Miss Hazel Giles. I think there were about 20 pupils with about half each of girls and boys. My first desk mate was Junior Turner. Our first lessons that I remember were arithmetic adding and subtraction, writing the alphabet with capital and lower case letters within parallel lines and reading. Miss Giles would demonstrate on a black board in front of the class and then have a student write on the black board. I had already done these lessons during first grade in Danville.

We had a recess period mid morning and another mid afternoon. There were two toilets separated some distance in back. The one for boys had a long, sloping trough made of wood boards as a urinal and 3 or 4 holes in a low bench for defecating. I never saw the inside of the girl's toilet, and the boys were warned to stay some distance away. Also in back was a mountain-size pile of firewood. During the fall when the woodpile was the largest, we boys would build little Igloo-type huts to crawl into.

There were several large oak trees in front of the elementary and high school buildings, and there was a hand pump on a concrete slab over a well. The rest of the front yard to the road was open and used as a playground. One area was a clay basketball court and another was a base ball diamond. The rest was for other games with balls, running, pop-the-whip, jump rope etc. Our recesses did not include organized team play or games but did require teacher supervision. One of Uncle Fletcher's quoted sayings "Unsupervised children should be a criminal offense" was true in some of the bullying and hazing of younger boys by older ones.

My experience with this involved my clothes. In rural 1931 nearly all families with school children were poor, and they were dressed as farmers; bib overalls and calico dresses all year and in the fall and spring most children went barefoot. Mother had Paul and me wear dress shoes all year, knee-length socks and shorts or nickers with a long-sleeve shirt. I was really picked on as being a "show-off and highfaluting." Mother gave no slack. Also, the large oak trees were used by two older boys to "buck" a defenseless smaller one by each picking him up by an arm and a leg facing up then swinging him repeatedly so his butt struck the tree. Usually the "bucked" boy would have a painful and bruised behind.

During one recess when I was being teased and bucked, a high school boy, Len Craddock, threatened my attackers and warned them to not bother me again. He then picked me up onto his shoulders and walked away toward the elementary building. I don't remember having anymore serious problems with teasing or bucking, and Mother did finally give in to long khaki trousers and bare feet during warm weather.

Another use for the oak trees in addition to bucking and shade was for dusting blackboard erasers. When the gray-felt erasers had collected so much chalk from erasing writing on the board that they would just smear the chalk and not leave a clean black surface, Miss Giles would select a pupil to take them out and beat them against the trees to clean them of the chalk. One day I was selected. On my return I stumbled on the front steps and cut my chin and was a little dazed. Miss Giles bandaged my chin and asked if someone would volunteer to copy my homework assignment for me. Wow! The prettiest girl in the class, Jewel Fox, raised her hand and seemed really happy. She was so pretty and self confident that I had been too shy to talk to her. I thanked her when she brought her paper and spoke to me. I think that was the highlight of my life to that point. I don't remember much more about second grade other than the discipline Miss Giles used for talkative children. One was to have her left hand hold the offending child's four fingers so that their palm was stretched flat then give a few strokes with a ruler across it until it turned red – just before a blister. The other punishment was to close the offender in the wood closet until the offender could decide to behave properly.

Spring of 1932 came along with a lot of bare feet and some of the pupils missing school to help plant tobacco. Then summer with school out and a lot of things to do and learn on the farm.

Paul and I had outdoor chores of cutting grass with a push reel-and-blade lawnmower around the house and with a scythe for long weeds farther away along paths to the out house, spring, chicken house and pig pen. Mother got a couple of shoats and a milk cow from Uncle Doug so we learned to feed the pigs with kitchen scraps and dish water mixed with "ship stuff" from ground wheat. Mother named our beige Guernsey-Jersey cross cow Buttercup. She had horns, and there was one little boy she did not seem to like. Mother milked her before breakfast and before supper each day. Paul was taught how to milk and feed her, and he started helping in the evenings. Once she was tied securely, I tried to learn to milk, but the milk went the wrong way back into her udder. Buttercup would become irritated with my efforts and start kicking her back foot on my arms and hands putting bedding into the milk bucket and overturning it. I was a hopeless student of milking and was given more work in the vegetable garden and looking after the chickens.

Daddy was still working for the bank in Danville so Paul and I spent a lot of time with Clyde. We learned how he would feed, catch, harness, hitch Dan to plows and wagons and then drive him to do what the job required. Clyde started letting us do some of the work, and sometimes he would put us on Dan's back with Paul in front to ride back to the stable from the field. Dan's backbone was like a 3" pipe above his body and became painful to sit on for very long. One time riding home down a steep hill, Paul slid forward over Dan's shoulder and along his neck before stopping at his ears. Going up the other side of the hill Paul was able to push himself back into riding position. With us having short legs riding a bumping big horse was not a really enjoyable experience for me.

Clyde continued to do farm and garden work, but he did not raise tobacco. He continued to do some building, including a new stable to replace the rotting log one. He was strong and knew how to cut trees into logs, stack the lumber to dry and season straight, cut the large beams and smaller framing ones to correct length and assemble them vertical, level and square. Daddy would give him directions on what to build and how to build, and leave for his job in Danville. When he returned in the evening, Daddy would check Clyde's progress and then give instructions for further work. The stable was to have two stalls for horses or cows on each side of a central alley which was to be used to put feed into a feed box or hay rack in each stall. Narrow boards nailed across studs at the end of the alley served as a ladder through an opening to the hay loft above. Daddy was helping frame the loft and roof when one end of a long rafter fell and hit Clyde in the head. Clyde was knocked down and had a deep gash in his head with a lot of blood. Daddy got him into the car and to Dr. Parrish in Chatham where he was treated and the cut in his head stitched. I think Clyde continued doing light work while his stitches healed.

There was a strong disagreement between Daddy and Clyde on one part of how the stable should be constructed. Clyde became very angry, said he was quitting and went home. He came back after a day off and asked for his job back. I think Mother and Daddy were glad to have him back at work.

A medicine show came to Mr. Billy Bowen's store at Climax and had shows on his porch in the evenings. His porch was raised to be a convenient loading dock at the same height as the store entrance, so it was a good stage for the show. Clyde was planning to go and he and Mother agreed he could take me. I don't know why Paul didn't go. It was late in the day when the show started with music and a few jokes by the "actors." Then came a sales speech for their "cure-all" tonic. A number of common ailments were guaranteed to be cured by a daily or more frequent dose of the tonic. The salesmen moved among the crowd of people distributing the sold bottles. Then there were a few more jokes and string music. The jokes were about the comical ignorance of colored people. One I remember part of was a blindfolded colored man trying to identify the tree by the smell of a branch from the tree. The lead actor would hold a branch under the nose of the blindfolded subject, and the subject would guess the name of the tree. He got a couple right, and then a dog's tail was held under his nose. His answer was, "dogwood" to great laughter from the crowd. Music, camaraderie and laughter among the audience drinking the "tonic" ended the show. It was dark when Clyde and I walked home.

Daddy was nearly finished clearing the bank accounts and distributing the assets with the court's approval during the spring of 1933. A lot of the settled accounts were mortgages held by or through the Federal Land Bank in Baltimore, Maryland. Their manager of these accounts was very favorably impressed with the work Daddy had done and offered him the position of Assistant Secretary of the Federal Land Bank. It was a good job with probable future advancement. I don't know what Mother and Daddy thought about his working in Baltimore, but he did go for an interview and introduction. Sometime during this decision-making period, his Uncle, Brigadier General, Retired, Edward (Ned) Anderson came from Florida to visit his local family and only living brother, Uncle Charlie. On his way past our house, he, his wife, Aunt Amelie, and their two children stopped for a short visit with us. Aunt Amelie was much younger than Uncle Ned, and she was very beautiful. Their two children, Fannie and Edward, were about Paul's and my age. They did not stay long so I mainly watched while Fannie, Edward , Katie and Paul talked. After they were gone, I heard Daddy tell Mother that Uncle Ned strongly advised him to take the job in Baltimore. That summer, Daddy went to work at the Federal Land Bank in Baltimore. He got an apartment there and would ride the train home and back every two weeks for a weekend stay. I think this was the plan until he could get better situated financially.

When school started in the fall, it was just Mother, we three children and Clyde and Maisie at Windcrest. My third grade teacher was

Miss Hazel Bennett. (*It was school policy to only employ women as teachers who were single*). She was young and small but as "tough as nails" and well qualified using a long switch. Long trousers were no hindrance because she had the boys pull the trouser legs up above their knees to expose bare skin. She was "Miss Discipline with a capital D." The only switching I remember her giving me was when Junior Smith and I were late getting back from the nearby Walker's Store after our lunch period. We shared a two-pupil desk and both of us were switched at the same time across our backs as we leaned over the desk. I don't remember much else about that part of my time in the third grade with Miss Bennett except some discussions about the presidential election campaigns and the result between Herbert Hoover and Franklin D. Roosevelt. Sometime around the first of January the pupil numbers in the two third grade classes became uneven. Miss Fleetwood Adams taught the other class and requested me as one of the pupils to be transferred to her class. In comparison to Miss Bennett, she was "nice as pie." I think I actually learned something in her class.

Near the end of third grade during recess boys in my class and older would talk about girls. They said that every month girls would wear rags in their panties to catch the blood that came from their female parts. They really seemed to know what they were talking about when two or three agreed and said that the girls would wash the rags and use them again. A new and something so unimaginable to me that my mind became fixated on such a possibility. I didn't even know what a pu**y looked like. The only time I had looked for Jean Yarborro's I didn't see anything. I wanted to ask a girl if it was true, but I was too embarrassed to do so.

The boys talked about "jerking off" and how good it felt. I had never heard about that before, but it seemed easy to do and did not require anyone else to help or know about. Later at home and away from the house, I tried doing what the boys said, and a new revelation of pleasure and addiction was opened.

In the spring we had a "May Day" festival. There was a May Pole with many different colored ribbons hanging from the top to the ground. An alternate girl and boy holding a ribbon would practice at recess singing something like, "Around and around the May Pole we dance in the Merry Month of May" as we skipped around the pole alternately going over and under the next ribbon until the pole was completely weaved with ribbons. Then the hard part of going in the opposite direction to unweave the ribbons. Sometimes a disaster. There were foot races between boys and between girls in each grade. I think Fannie Foust was the girl winner and Taz Anderson the boy in our grade. There were chinning bar contests, catch the greasy pig, climb the greasy pole, sometimes a baseball game and horse racing. Several dare-devil local riders put on a show before the race. One in particular was Larry Reynolds who seemed on the verge of being drunk. He rode his horse around with some rearing and sort of dancing. I think he came in first or second.

Larry's brother Ben was in Paul's grade on the second floor. He was expelled for putting bullets in the unlighted heater in his room. The bullets went off when the fire got hot and scared everyone on the second floor. Ben had three older brothers Larry, Randall and Gerald. Gerald was the oldest and lived on his father's, Booker's, farm with his wife and children. Randall was married too and a dentist in Chatham.

Someone, I think Howard Woody, came on an Indian motorcycle and gave me a ride to the store and back. A Piper Cub airplane came from Danville and charged a small amount for short rides from the field next to the school. There were lots of people who came and brought special food for sale. This was a big celebration just before the end of the school year and the beginning of a hard, continuous and hot farming summer for most children and their families.

On summer evenings after supper we would sit on our front porch and listen to insects chirping, and in the early evening whip-o-wills call. Sometimes we would hear a barn owl "Who" or a screech owl scream. Most evenings a little toad would hop from the grass onto the rock steps. It wasn't really tame, but we could catch and hold it. He was a "regular" so we named him Ferdinand. They were silent evenings. We could hear the train whistle at the Whittles crossing nearly 10 miles away and the rumble of the steel wheels against the rails as it rolled toward Chatham. Most evenings we would sing hymns. Some evenings when we finished a song, the Bowen family across the hollow would sing a different hymn. Our next song then would be louder. Then they would try to make theirs even louder. After a few hymns of competition we gave out of competition and would shout, "Good Night." It did not take long for us to get sleepy and ready for bed.

During the 1929-1934 financial depression in Pittsylvania County, many people, especially farmers, suffered through poverty, and lost their property through defaulted mortgages. Many farmers borrowed money in the spring for seed and fertilizer and for an account at the local general store for food. There were a few men with money or credit who used their wealth and influence to become wealthy. Uncle Hurt was the majority stockholder and President of Planters Bank in Chatham which owned mortgages on many family farms. Uncle Hurt was of an aristocratic family which was expected to conduct business in a way most profitable to the business. Uncle Hurt did, and increased his wealth in the process. As each farm mortgage became due, credit was not extended and the bank foreclosed on the mortgage and became owner of the farm. Uncle Hurt then bought the farm for the amount owed and allowed the family to continue living on the farm as tenants or sharecroppers. As children during those times, their were few secrets that were not compromised. One was the boasts by Uncle Hurt's children that he owned 120 farms. A reputation of pride as a good business man. Other men who owned general stores or had money did the same. A similar situation happened to Daddy, but a different outcome.

The Federal Land Bank owned the defaulted mortgage on a farm near our farm that he wanted for it's proximity and good tobacco soil. Instead of using other men's acquisition process, Daddy waited until one of his weekend home visits to find and purchase the farm from the owner at a fair price above the mortgage amount. By the time he found the owner it was too late. Another neighbor had capitalized on the owner's addiction to whiskey and bought the farm from the drunken owner.

Shortly after we moved to Windcrest Daddy had a telephone installed. His first cousin, Frank Anderson, owned the Tomahawk Telephone Company. He and his two older sons, Roger and Harold, erected the poles, ran the wires, installed the telephones and did the maintenance work. His second wife, Thelma, ran the switch board in their home. The poles were small locust trees cut to hold the wire on glass insulators about 15 feet above the ground. Roger and Harold dug the holes for the poles with hand diggers, planted the poles tightly by tamping dirt in the hole around the pole then climbing a ladder to attach the insulator and wire. Tomahawk Telephone Company served a large area in the Five Points and Climax area, but I think they did not have an abundance of customers because of the low population density. We had a hand crank, wall-mounted model with a note shelf over an open cubbyhole box, and we were connected to a party line with other customers. To distinguish a call to a phone from others on our line, each customer was assigned a different ring signal. I think ours was two shorts and a long. Everyone on our line could hear what anyone else said just by picking up their receiver and listening. I don't think there was an honor system, so it was assumed that others were listening to your conversation. To make a call to Chatham required a connection through the switchboard.

Another early improvement to our comfort was a well near the house to take the place of the spring. Daddy made an agreement with three black men to hand dig a well close to our long side porch. Brothers Hayes, Andrew and Forty Hubbard were sharecroppers on the Rorer farm along Pigg River about 6 miles from us. Hayes was the oldest and was in charge of the work. Forty was the youngest and smallest. They started by cutting off the handles of their digging tools, pick, shovel, mattock, sledge hammer to the length that would allow their use in the 3-ft. diameter hole they would dig. They made a bucket from a 25-pound wood nail keg by bending a hickory limb over the top and fastening each end to the sides with nails. Their windless was made from three boards for each end by crossing two into an X and fastening the third to join the bottom ends. These two ends were then placed upright about 4 feet apart and joined at the bottom and along the sides with several boards to form the base of the windless. A six-inch-diameter pole was fitted with a "cranking" handle at each end with each handle attached in the opposite direction of the other. This was then placed on the windless base in the upright crossed boards. One end of a long rope was attached to the middle of the turning pole and the other end was tied to the nail-keg bucket. The digging began. The three men worked in shifts with one digging and filling the bucket in the well and the other two operating the windless to pull up the full bucket, emptying it and returning it down to the digger. When we returned from school each day, we would look into the well to see how deep they had gotten. They got to about 20 feet within a week or two, but then came to hard sandstone against which their pick and mattock were not very useful. I think their agreement included a payment when they reached water and the final payment when they had dug an additional 10 feet. With the uncertainty of how thick this rock was and during the depression with no other money available, they decided to continue.

The brothers got a hardened 1 ½" diameter steel rod about 3' long and sharpened in an "X"on one end as a "drill" and pounded this into the rock to make a hole about 2 feet deep. A stick of dynamite with a percussion cap and long fuse was lowered into the hole. Forty, being the smallest, was chosen to light the fuse and then be rapidly pulled up by

Hayes and Andrew who then picked up the windless and moved it away from the blast. The explosion was deafening like a cannon being fired. The ground and house shook, rocks, dust and smoke came flying out of the well hole and into the air higher than the house and rocks falling on the roof and into the yard for some fifty feet around.

One day when we were not in school, we got to watch the blasting operation. I think Hayes and Andrew decided to put on a special show for us. Katie would not watch and went to her room upstairs, but Paul and I watched at a distance from the well while Forty was lowered in the bucket to light the fuse. Forty lit the fuse jerked on the rope and shouted, " All right it's lit, pull me up." Hayes and Andrew just stood, and Hayes shouted back, "What did you say?" Forty excitedly shouted back, "Pull me up I got it lit." Then Hayes and Andrew started turning the windless as fast as they could. When Forty got to the top, he was out of the bucket and started running. Hayes and Andrew were laughing heartily as they lifted the windless and started running too. They had not gotten far before the blast scattered rocks all around. Hayes and Andrew continued laughing, but I think Forty had turned a little pale. I had been scared and I did not laugh.

To clear the dynamite smoke and dust from the well, the trunk of a small pine was tied to the rope in place of the bucket and let down and up repeatedly. Then they would wait a day or two to repeat the blasting process. The digging and blasting went on for a month or more before water was finally reached. The work was even harder by having to remove water and also dig, but the three Hubbards were happier with some money and the promise of getting more soon. Paul and I were happy too with the prospect of an endless supply of water and no more trips to the spring and back.

The wall of the upper 20 feet of the well was lined with flat rocks, and a concrete slab was put around the top. A grooved wheel pulley was attached to a cross beam over a box-like housing over the well, and a bucket was fastened to each end of a chain over the pulley. I could bring up a bucket full of water and close the hinged top to support the full bucket, but I was not big or strong enough to pour the water into another bucket to take into the house.

The price of tobacco was so low that Daddy did not make any effort to have any raised on his "Lower Place" 65 acres or on Mother's "Home Place" 90 acres. I think the sale price at the tobacco markets in Danville varied around 5 and 10 cents per pound. After Roosevelt was elected President, farmers were encouraged to form cooperatives to set acreage allotment for each farm and by setting these limits on production to only supply the amount tobacco companies would need to meet their needs, The federal government would guarantee a minimum sale price based on the quality grade of the tobacco sold. The tobacco bought by the government was stored in warehouses and used in helping determine the next year's production allotments. Tobacco farmers overwhelmingly approved the plan, and local committees were elected to manage the allotment process.

On the home place there was no extra house for anyone to live, but there was a three-room "tenant" house near a spring on the lower place. Daddy made arrangements to have a sharecropper live there and raise tobacco on both farms. There were curing and pack barns on both farms, and each also had stripping rooms and "ordering" pits. Daddy traded Dan for two matched mules, Pat and Jack, and he bought a two-horse wagon, turning plow, hay mower and wheat drill. A family moved into the lower place house and started farming. The first tobacco acreage was very small because the main criteria for determining allotments was based on a three-year average of previous acreage, and our farms had not raised any during that time. I watched as the sharecropping family tended their crops of tobacco, corn and hay. At near tobacco harvest, the lowest leaves would turn yellow before any of the upper leaves. They were picked individually put in a mule-drawn sled with high sides of burlap bags and taken to a curing barn where they were held in bunches by children while an adult tied them onto tobacco sticks and hung the sticks across tier poles inside the barn. They were cured by having the hot gases from a wood fire in a long rock and mud furnace pass through a flue pipe rising slightly across the dirt floor of the barn to the back and turning back to the front of the barn to exhaust outside. When the leaves turned to the desired yellow color and dried, the fire was put out and the leaves allowed to pick up enough moisture from the night air to be flexible, they were moved still tied to sticks to a pack barn. By then the leaves on the rest of the tobacco stalk had ripened to a yellow color, and a semicircle-shaped knife sharp on both edges was used to split the standing stalk down the middle from top to near bottom. The stalk was cut off at ground level, pulled apart at the slit and hung upside down over a stick being held by another person. These were put on a wagon and hauled to a curing barn and cured the same way as the previously cured leaves.

After this first tobacco crop, a new variety of tobacco with leaves to be picked as they ripened from bottom to top of the stalk was planted. Children could be used more to harvest the new type of tobacco because it did not require holding and handling the heavy stalks.

Chapter 5

Slowly Forward

"Experience is, for me, the highest authority. The touchstone of validity is my own experience. ... Neither the Bible nor the prophets --- neither Freud nor research --- neither the revelations of God nor man --- can take precedence over my own direct experience."

Carl Rogers

There was always building, repairing or maintaining something. Clyde was good at these jobs, but there were some that required more time and skill than Clyde had. Malcolm's and Jack's daddy, Mr. John Adkins was a skilled carpenter and rock and concrete mason. Mr. Adkins built tall rock pillars on each side of the entrance to our driveway, a large rock headstone containing an engraved marble plaque for Daddy's mother's and daddy's grave in the family cemetery and a new three- room frame tenant house fronting on the main road and not far from our house. Mr. Adkins and Clyde built the house and the rock chimney with fire place, and Clyde, Maisie and their baby moved in. Often Malcolm and Jack would come with their daddy to work and to play with us. The usable logs from Clyde's old house were moved to our back yard and re assembled into a story-and a-half summer and guest house by Mr. Adkins and Clyde. They also built a chimney with a fireplace having a swinging steel arm to hold a pot.

Other building projects included a large combination garage, machinery and wheat storage building. Also, there were chicken houses and utility and smoke houses.

All of these buildings required more lumber than Clyde could furnish from trees on our farm. Daddy hired a neighbor, Lonnie Gibson, to selectively cut trees and haul them to a saw mill and bring the lumber to be stacked for drying. Lonnie would select trees that were large enough for sawing into lumber and the kind of tree for the kind of lumber needed. Mostly poplar for weather boarding and pine for structural framing. He made an effort to not harm the remaining small and unneeded trees. To do this, he had a team of four mules harnessed in a single file that could be guided around the "saved" trees. I watched as he and his oldest son used a two-man crosscut saw to cut the trees down and then cut them into the desired lengths as logs. One log at a time was chained to the mules and dragged through the standing trees and up a hill to be loaded onto a wagon. Because the dragging path was so narrow, Lonnie walked behind the mules and guided the lead mule with only one reign line. He alternately threw the reign from one side tho the other as the path turned.

All of this was of much interest to me and educational for later times when a little more lumber was needed. Clyde needed another person to use the two-man (-boy) saw. Paul or I was the boy. When my turn came, I found out that it was not truly a boy's job, but the experience was of much use later when I was a man.

Additions to our house were made by a more experienced and professional carpenter, Mr Sam Reynolds. He and his son Harry enclosed and finished the interior of the long side porch into a family/sun room. There were windows all along the south side, and the interior walls were paneled with beaded, wide boards of clear-shellacked knotty pine. They also covered the interior walls of the rest of the house with the new fire-retardant building material, gypsum board,(sheet rock). I think the most appreciated by Paul and me was a new room for us over the kitchen with back stairs from the dinning room. We had been sleeping in the room over the dining room, and Mother slept in the front bed room. She then took our room and left her room for a guest room. These and other building projects were a continuing process over several years.

Greenpond Baptist Church had been constituted in 1865 and a building was constructed on land donated by Daddy's grandfather, Watt Otey Anderson. Daddy's Crider Grandfather was a Methodist minister, and his Crider kin were Methodists, but Daddy's mother was an Anderson, and when he married into the Whitehead Baptist family, he was married by a Baptist minister and joined the Baptist Church in Chatham. All of his Anderson family were Baptists. I do not remember going to church in Chatham and only once to the Baptist Church in Danville, but from the first Sunday at Windcrest we attended Greenpond. The preacher at church was Mr. J. D. Kessler. He, his mother and his children, Dorothy, Dan, Ruth and Jack lived in the parsonage house next to the church. Mr. Kessler's wife had died. Dorothy was the oldest, Dan a little older than Katie, Ruth Paul's age and in his class at school and Jack a year younger than me. There was Sunday School every Sunday, but because of the depression, Greenpond shared the preacher and his salary with Hollywood Baptist Church about 5 miles away. We had preaching every other Sunday.

The church building was a big wood-frame white building with two front doors each with steps, one for women and the other for men. Inside there was a tall ceiling with exposed beams and roof rafters, an isle along each side and one down the middle of rows of wooden pews. White cotton sheets with rings were hung from several wires suspended from the beams. The sheets were pulled to form classrooms during Sunday School and opened for church service. There were two large wood-burning heaters, one on each side near the front of the audience and close to the raised pulpit platform and choir loft behind.

Mr. Kessler was a "fire and brimstone" preacher talking about a camel going through a needle's eye to get into heaven, wives submitting to their husbands and the sermons about God watching all the time everything little boys did and about the sin of spilling their seed on the ground instead of making babies put a heavy load of guilt on me. Even though I wasn't spilling seed, I was doing what he was talking about. Mr. Kessler was an energetic, loud speaker. He would wave his arms and use his arms and hands to point at the audience, and it seamed directly at me when making a point about spilling seed.

Mr. Kessler's sermons scared me into shame and repentance, but not into abstinence; just shame and secrecy.

I think after Paul had finished fifth grade he went forward one night during the summer revival when the preacher called for sinners to come forward, repent and give their life to Jesus. I did not know if I should do that or not, but Mother said I was too young. I think she was right.

Katie, Paul and I each got a bicycle our first Christmas at Windcrest. It was hard work for me to ride mine on rough and rutted roads, but later in the spring and summer we would ride to the Kessler's and play with them in the church parking lot and a game with one team on one side of their house and another on the opposite side. A member on one would shout, " Ally, Ally Oop" and throw a ball over the house for a member on the opposite side of the house to catch. The side to catch most balls would be the winner.

Sometimes Dan and Ruth would walk to our house. I think Jack was not allowed to come because he was too young. Sometimes we just played there, and sometimes we would walk to the mill pond and swim. Dan and Paul could swim and dive from the gate mechanism at the dam. Katie, Ruth and I watched them and then walked to the shallow part near the incoming Tomahawk Creek. We would wade in there and walk along the bottom and try to float and swim. Dan, Paul and I just took our shoes and shirts off to swim in shorts. I don't remember how the girls dressed.

One morning at breakfast soon after I had been transferred to Miss Adam's classroom, Clyde came in with an armful of firewood and said that there would not be any school that day. He continued to tell how just a little after sundown he had seen the skyline light up in the direction of the school and walked there and saw the school burning. When he got there, the high school and elementary school buildings were both burning so hot that no one could get close or do anything to try to put the fire out.

He said that the brick auditorium building and the caretaker's house did not burn. I was glad that I did not have to go to school, but Katie and Paul were not as happy. Mother asked if anyone knew how the fire started, and Clyde said that some people at the fire said they thought it may have been spontaneous combustion from paint and oily rags left in a classroom on the second floor. Katie said that some men had been painting in her seventh grade room and had left some rags, cans of brush-cleaning liquid and buckets of paint in the closet of her classroom. Later, the county fire marshal decided that the fire was not started deliberately and most likely was started by spontaneous combustion from the confined oily rags and spread to the paint and paint-cleaning liquids.

It was not long before we were back in school. The auditorium building and caretaker's house were made into classrooms by putting in temporary walls and using part of the caretaker's house for a couple of classrooms. My new teacher in one of the rooms of the caretaker's house, Miss Inge, was really nice and was very helpful trying to teach. School was soon out for the summer, and I was glad.

That summer cousin Otha Hudson took us and four of his children, Billy, Rodney, Catherine and Jacqueline to an air show at the Danville airport. I think Mother gave each of us some money for admission and for food. There were three or four two-winged airplanes and several different acts announced over a loudspeaker. One was a fast, low-flying plane just a few feet over the runway and a person standing on the middle of the top wing. At the end of the runway, the airplane would make a wide turn into a little higher return pass over the runway, and the person on the wing would wave her streaming scarf to the applauding and cheering crowd. Another was a demonstration of skywriting. The airplane high in the sky started leaving a white smoke trail and made turns to write script words, *air show.* Then there were daring steep climbs, loops, dives turning back up just before crashing and tailspins. Two planes coming from opposite ends of the runway would bank in opposite directions and turn for a near miss as they roared by the clapping and shouting crowd. That was a very exciting day for me.

Later in the summer Cousin Otha took us to Smith Mountain to pick huckleberries. We had a few small buckets that two or three children shared to put berries in, and after being warned about poison oak and moccasin and rattle snakes, we went along paths leading up the mountain looking for huckleberries. We found and picked a lot of berries as each group went along different paths up the mountain. A medium-size snake crawled from under low bushes and across our path. I was very scared and and started screaming, "Snake, Snake." The other two children with me repeatedly shouted to me, " Shut up, shut up, its only a black snake." Cousin Otha had heard me and came as fast as he could with his rifle. He was told that it was only a black snake that had rapidly crawled away. Cousin Otha did not say much, but told us to bring our buckets and go to the car. Everyone was quiet on our way home except for Paul who told me how dumb I was. I felt really bad and wanted to cry.

Each July Greenpond would have a week-long revival and homecoming. A visiting preacher would come and give sermons Monday through Saturday evenings, and the choir would sing special hymns. The last and closing day on Sunday celebrated the sinners converted during the revival, the homecoming visitors and a big picnic meal after the sermon. The homecoming visitors were former church members who had moved away and were back visiting their family and friends. The picnic was a happy party with friends and family. Each family brought special food, and there were lots of watermelon, cantaloupe, cakes, pies, cup cakes, ice tea and lemonade. Children ran and played between trips to the long food-laden tables under the oak trees in the church yard. Katie, Paul and several other children had been "saved" and would be baptized the next Sunday afternoon after church service.

In addition to the failure of the bank where Daddy worked, there were some local people who lost their jobs in cities where they had gone to work. There were some children at school whose daddies brought their families back to the home farm to live and get support from family members. A couple of them were living in unused log tobacco barns and attached pack houses. Daddy's first cousin, Bruce Anderson, lost his engineering job in Michigan and brought his wife and six children to live at his mother's farm. The children were six boys ages from 4 to 16. Bruce's daddy, Great Uncle Dr. John Anderson was dead, but there was a closed store near his widow mother's home that was used as a residence for them. Sheets divided the large first and second floor rooms into smaller "rooms".

Bruce had brothers and sisters who helped furnish some of their needs, and Greenpond Church members took up collections of food, clothing and a little money for them. We had two milk cows, and Mother loaned one to them to use during her milking cycle. Bruce and his family came to Sunday School and church regularly. Bruce was assigned as teacher of the young boy's Sunday School class. The lesson he taught about Moses leading the Israelites across the Red Sea while fleeing the Egyptian Army seemed to stray from the traditional miracle intervention of God. According to Bruce: when Moses and his followers got to the banks of the Red Sea which was blocking their escape, a natural wind storm with a powerful downdraft blew the shallow waters apart to leave a path from shore to shore. The storm did not last long, but it was long enough for all of the Israelites to safely cross before the water closed and blocked the pursuing Egyptian Army. A vivid revelation to me.

I only remember visiting Bruce's children once. Paul and I walked a path instead of the longer road. When we got close, we could hear Bruce and his wife screaming in a terrible argument. Some of the children were outside, and we talked some and then went inside for a short time and then up to their grandmother's house. Aunt "Molly" lived alone, but some of her grandchildren usually spent the night with her. The day Paul and I were there, her son, Dr. John C. Anderson, Jr., was there. He and his mother had a good humor discussion about cousin John's experience as a WW Army doctor. She said that the reason he became an Army doctor was so he could practice operating on wounded soldiers. That he wanted experience doing amputations and sewing up bayonet cuts which were things he did not get to do in Medical School. He responded that he was a better doctor than most as a result of that learning.

Clyde planted field peas in a field bordering the pasture and along the road. They grew into long vines that needed to stacked on pyramid-type open pole frames in order for them to dry for hay. One night Dan got over the pasture fence and ate a lot of the drying pea vines. The next day his belly was bloated, and he was lying on his side groaning. Dr. Allen, the veterinarian in Chatham, came and drenched him with some kind of oil and stuck a cannula through his belly to let the bloating gas out. The treatments did not make Dan well, and shortly after standing up for a while he died.

When Daddy bought two mules to replace Dan, Uncle Doug sent two little Hampshire female pigs to Paul and me. Clyde had made a little pen for them before we got home from school. Mother had a big surprise for us. She told Paul and me to go down and look in a little pen at the back of the stable to see what was in it. Paul and I saw two of the cutesiest little pigs and the first ones we had seen up close and could touch. Both were black with a white stripe from one front foot up the leg, across their back and down the other leg. One had a little wider stripe than the other. We ran back to the house and excitingly laughing and jumping told Mother what we saw. She then told us that Uncle Doug had given Paul and me the Hampshire pigs, and that we were to each have one and look after it. They were really little pigs, so Mother gave us each a baby bottle with nipple and milk to feed the pig we chose. Paul named his Pat, and I named mine Sue. We gathered leaves and straw for bedding and spent a lot of time after school just watching them play with each other.

Pat and Sue grew fast, and we gradually weaned them from the bottle to regular pig feed. Clyde made a V-shaped trough from two planks and ends from short boards. We could feed wet feed in it, dry feed in a small wood open-top box and water in a bucket tied against the fence to keep it from turning over. About 3 or 4 weeks after we got Pat and Sue, Uncle Hurt sent to Paul and me a small male Hampshire pig. We named him WP for me and Paul. I don't know why Paul agreed to put my name first. All three pigs grew fast and soon needed a larger pen which we helped Clyde build with one side as the side of the machinery building nearer our house.

Mother did not drive our car, but one evening she wanted to go to the local organizing meeting of an electric cooperative at Climax School. This was under the Rural Electric Administration, REA, established by

President Franklin Roosevelt under a low-interest long-term federal loan to the cooperative. Daddy had bought a one-horse buggy with a folding top and rain side and front removable rain curtains. After an early supper, Mother had Clyde hitch one of the mules to the buggy and hang a kerosene lantern on the back. I was chosen to go with her. I think Paul had homework. When we went, it was still daylight so we did not light the lantern. Someone tied our mule to a fence in front of the Agriculture building, and we went inside. There were a lot of men there, and they had a speaker from nearby in Mecklenburg County that wanted us to join their cooperative and would include the area around Gretna and east to where it would meet them. Membership requirements, fees and estimated monthly service costs were discussed, and then an application form was circulated for people to sign. Mother signed, and by then it was dark. Mother lit the lantern hanging on the back of the buggy, and we rode home. I don't remember much about the evening after getting home. I probably fell asleep on my way to bed.

Paul and I were chronic bed-wetters: not every night, but often. I think every remedy anyone suggested to Mother was tried. Nothing was effective. Waking up in a wet and smelly bed felt really bad and made me want to not have that happen anymore. I tried to help make each suggested method or home medication work. Eating sour sumac seed, sheep sorrel and vinegar on sugar: no water or liquids at least an hour before going to bed and using the chamber pot just before getting into bed. Some of these seemed to help, but none resulted in a cure. I think I was potty trained at a normal age, but the bed wetting continued. I don't remember Katie having this problem; just Paul and me. On hot spring and fall days at school, a few of the boys would smell of urine. After Paul or I wet the bed, Mother made us "sponge bath" to take the odor away.

When school started in the fall, a new one story brick building had been built on the place where the old elementary building had been. A large new white wood-frame building for Agriculture class in front and a large building with big doors in back for shop was built where the old high school building had been. A new house for the caretaker was built a little ways behind the Agriculture building, and his old house was used for Home Economics. My fourth grade teacher was Miss Annie White who had all the fourth grade pupils in her class. Each pupil had a desk and chair, and there were tall windows along one side facing the front of the building. In arithmetic we were learning multiplication tables and division both of which I was having a lot of trouble. I knew all the children in my class and was glad that Jewel Fox was there. She was the prettiest girl I had ever seen, and she seemed to like me. She had big round blue eyes, nice large front teeth, brown hair and a really nice smile. I think she made good grades too. I was really nervous talking to her. We boys were big enough to start trying to play marbles and mumble peg. In back of the school there were some reed-like bushes with jointed stalks having pith centers. We would cut small stalks into lengths about a foot long, use a stick to push the pith out and use it as a blow gun to shoot spit balls at each other. Some of the boys in higher grades shot some at their teacher while she was writing on the black board and had her back turned. I think the ones that she caught got paddled by the principal.

After we moved to Windcrest, Sallie continued teaching at Schoolfield Elementary School and was boarding with Cousin Dr. Howell

Watson and his wife Alma in Danville during the school year. She came to live with us on the farm during the summer. She met and started dating a neighbor, Larry Reynolds. He had finished high school at Climax and was farming on his father's farm about four miles from where we lived. I knew him from the visits he made to the school during May Day festivals. Entered his horse in the racing competition and made a show with riding and rearing his horse around the school grounds during stages of drunkenness.

Larry's father, Booker T. Reynolds, owned and farmed a large acreage using his sons and sharecroppers. Gerald, the oldest and married with children, lived and farmed part of his father's farm. Randall was the next oldest, had graduated from the Richmond School of Dentistry and had a thriving practice in Chatham. Larry was next, and Ben was the youngest son and still going to Climax High School. Larry had the reputation of being the wildest of the four, and Gerald was the "ladies' man." Randall was a respected man with money and political influence. He became a director of Planters Bank and mayor of Chatham. When Gerald or Larry were in trouble, Randall always came to the rescue before serious legal charges could be prosecuted. Thus, no documented record of a lot of "word of mouth" scandals. And there were several that were very likely true.

When Larry was younger, he "borrowed" Randall's car for a "joy ride" at high speeds on dirt and gravel roads. No caution for road conditions or twists and turns. No traction around a sharp turn, and only stopped upside down in the ditch. Larry was injured, but nor critically. The only permanent visible record of the accident was a scar on the left side of his face. From his eyebrow, across the edge of his eye and down to his jaw. Otherwise, he was a handsome, tall and thin man with light brown hair and blue eyes. He was just who Sallie was attracted to, handsome, scar, reputation and character.

Dating Larry continued during Sallie's summer vacation which she spent at home on the farm with us. When Mother went to Baltimore for a visit, Larry came to visit Sallie at our house because she was responsible for we three younger children and could not go dating. He was jolly and took part in our family activities, even jokingly making fun of our childish ways. Near the end of summer, Sallie and Larry decided to get married.

Daddy came home and tried to convince Sallie to break the engagement. A lost cause with an independent "mature" adult. Larry was the wild, reckless, manly exciting partner Sallie needed to help her be who she wanted to be and to rebel against impossible conformity to Daddy's "good name and appearances." Daddy left. Larry came August, 1932 in Randall's borrowed car and took Sallie with him to be married in a clerk's office and then to live in a log cabin on another part of his father's farm. Off to a marriage and honeymoon without Daddy's consent and with Mother's hopes.

Two lovers living the carefree, wild and exciting life of irresponsibility came to a screeching halt with the words, "I do" at the clerk's office. A new start for Sallie. She moved into a log house on a 100-acre farm belonging to Larry's father. She was good at house keeping and decorating the rustic house, but not good at being a farmers' wife or taking direction. When ordered to milk their cow, she struggled to learn.

When she came with only half or less of the usual amount of milk, Larry demanded a better effort from her. She tried coy beguiling, but that did not succeed in this new married relationship. An impossible and repulsive task that she knew she could not meet. Her independent attitude could not be compromised. She put water in the milk bucket to bring the amount to "normal." Rifts between the two continued until fall when she returned to Danville to board with cousin Howell and Alma Watson and to teach school at Schoolfield Elementary.

Larry living alone on the farm with weekend visits from Sallie was not enough for him. And some weekends Sallie gave an excuse for not visiting him.

Except for a few exceptions, Paul and my lives during the summer were physically sharing the same home, but not as emotional friends. Paul was always the dominant, and I was self-satisfied doing things that interested me. One of his demonstrations proving his superior abilities was climbing one of the four large oak trees across the public road from our house. They were too large to reach around, but one had a large limb close enough to the ground that he could jump and grab his arms around and pull himself up to start his climb to near the top. After shouting and shaking a small limb, he came down.

Lou and her two-year-old daughter, Bobbie Lou, came for a summer vacation visit. Lou drove her dark-green two-door Model A Ford sedan and planned to stay a week. One day during her stay, Sallie came and said that she and Larry had a big argument and he threatened to cut her throat. When he left the house to work on the farm, she took some of her clothes and left to walk to our house. It was late in the day, and Sallie,

Lou and Mother talked a lot about what to do. Sallie thought Larry would come there looking for her, and she was afraid of what he might do to her. Mother asked if she was going to have a baby, and Sallie said she didn't think so that she didn't feel any thrills. Mother threw up her hands and said, "You Goose, don't you know how to tell?" I did not understand what they were saying after that until they started talking about how to get her away.

Finally, I was told that early the next morning I would go in Lou's car with her, Sallie and Bobbie Lou to Norfolk. I went to bed. Early the next morning, Mother had us up for breakfast, packed my clothes and lunch for all four of us. We also took a jar with a lid in case I couldn't hold my need to pee until the next picnic rest stop. Lou did not make many stops, and was alert for any cars approaching us from behind for fear Larry might find out about us and try to catch up with us. We stopped for gas and then at a picnic table for a quick lunch and a walk on separate paths for men and women through bushes to a place away from the road to pee. There was not much talking, and Bobbie and I slept some. We finally came to Portsmouth and the ferry terminal to Norfolk. I became interested then watching the cars drive onto the ferry deck and some people walk on and sit on benches. The ferry blew a horn, closed the entrance gate and started toward the Norfolk terminal. The people walked off, the exit gate was opened and the cars drove onto the pier and on into the street. It did not take long to get to Lou's house. She fixed a place for Sallie and me to sleep and then she and Sallie fixed supper before Robert came home from work. I went to bed early.

The next morning Daddy came from Baltimore on the overnight

ferry. He stayed all day and talked a lot with Sallie and Lou. In the late afternoon I went with him to the Baltimore ferry pier. There were some cars that got on, and there were rooms with double deck beds. We took our bags of clothes to our room then went to a dining area to eat supper. The ferry got under way, and we watched the shore lights and lights from other boats and ships from the deck for awhile before I went to bed in the upper bunk. I went to sleep and don't remember Daddy coming in. The ship had docked when he woke me the next morning. We got dressed, left the ferry and caught a taxi to the B & O Rail Road Station in Baltimore. He bought a ticket to Chatham for me, and we had something for breakfast. He gave me instructions on how to change trains in Washington to the Southern Railway, gave me some money for food and Red Cap tips, helped me get on the train and left for work at the bank. The B & O trains north of Washington did not have separate cars for colored and white passengers. With the help of a Red Cap porter at the Washington central station I made my connection to the Southern whites-only car. It was a hot day and the windows were open a little to let air in. When we went into a tunnel under Alexandria, Virginia, black smoke poured in through the windows and left us passengers almost black enough to pass for travel on the colored cars. It was a long, shaky, clickity-clack rail joint noise, whistle-blowing road crossings and gritty all day trip with several station stops. When I arrived at the Chatham station and got off, it was late in the day. No one was there to meet me, so I asked the local taxi man, Vaden Moorman, if he would take me home and let mother pay him. He knew my family from his family having been sharecroppers on Daddy's mother's farm. It was just turning dark when he stopped at our front gate for me to get out.

I was nearly to the front door when our fox terrier cross guard dog, Tuffy, heard me shut the car door and came viciously barking and growling from in back of our house. I was afraid he might bite me before he recognized who I was and quickly got between the screen door and the front door. When I spoke his name to him, he went crazy with excitement to know it was me. Mother had heard Tuffy and was cautiously coming to the door when I turned the handle to ring the bell. She asked who was there and opened the door when I told her it was I. When we hugged each other, I started crying with my tears flowing like a river. I couldn't talk. I just finally felt safe again. Mother asked Vaden what was wrong, but he said he didn't know; I seemed alright. I knew, and nothing was wrong anymore. All was finally right.

Daddy traded our Model T Ford for a 1934 black Chevrolet sedan, and Mother decided that she needed to learn to drive. She hired Garland Anderson, Uncle Charlie's son, to teach her. Garland came for several lessons and finally had her using the clutch to shift gears from one to the next without scraping them. I don't think a driver's license was required, so after a few lessons with Mother driving and Garland in the seat beside her, he said that Mother was ready to drive by herself.

Chapter 6

Another World

**Irrationally held truths may be more
harmful than reasoned errors.**

Thomas Huxley

One summer afternoon Mother asked me to go with her to visit
Cousin Maude Easley who lived on a farm about three miles from us. I
was glad to go for a ride, especially since I was not required to wash my
feet and put on shoes. As we started down a steep curve to the left at the
intersection with another road, Mother pushed in the clutch which caused
the car to increase speed and excited her and me. She did not turn the
steering wheel fast enough to stay in the road and slid into a deep ditch on
my side. The high bank on my side kept us from turning over, but my
head hit something and knocked me unconscious. Some man in a car
stopped to help. Our car was leaning so steeply into the ditch that he had
to lift the door from outside to get Mother out and then pull me out. He
said that Edwin Smith had his truck with some chains just a short distance
away and he would get him to pull our car out of the ditch. He with the
help of a couple of other men with him pulled our car along the ditch to a
shallower part and then back into the road. Mother told Mr. Smith that
Garland told her to push the clutch in before putting on the brake, and
that is what she was doing when the car suddenly speeded up out of
control. Mr. Smith said that was only correct when you were going to
stop, not when you were going to slow down. Mother then asked Mr.
Smith if he would drive us home. He said that he would, but he strongly

advised against it because if she did not continue to where she had started, she probably would be afraid to drive again. She took his advice and drove us on to Cousin Maude's. I had a big knot on the right side of my head and a blue bruise.

Lou got TB and was sent for treatment to a sanitarium near Charlottesville. Even though Mother could drive around home, she did not want to try driving the 130 miles to Charlottesville. She made arrangements with Garland to drive her and me to see Lou. When we arrived at the TB sanitarium, only Mother was allowed to go in to see Lou. Garland and I sat in the car outside. Lou met mother in one of the sun rooms that had windows all along the walls, and they came to one of the windows and waved to Garland and me. When Mother came back to the car, she said that Lou was getting better, but would have to stay another few months for further treatment. When she would go home, she would have to continue to rest a lot and not exert herself. Also, she should not strain her system by having any more children.

That fall Mother had some kind of medical problem and needed to have surgery in a hospital in Baltimore and asked Cousin Maude to keep us three children. They had moved into a house across the road from Greenpond Church. They rented Cousin Janie Jones' farm and lived in a big two-story house with front and back porches. We could catch the school bus in front of their house which was close to the road. I was really nervous that I might wet her bed and tried not to drink much water and to pee in the chamber pot at bedtime. My bed had a thick feather tic that I sunk down into so far that it folded over me almost to cover my face and whole body. Soft and warm. I don't remember which night that I woke from in a soaking wet tic. I took off my pajamas and dried myself the best I could with the dry arms and legs and got dressed for school. At breakfast I told Cousin Maude I had wet the bed and that I had tried not to and was sorry. I am not sure what she said, but she was not mad. Paul did not wet his bed. I was really glad when Mother came home.

A couple of months after the Atlantic Coast hurricane, Daddy needed to go to Porto Rico to assess damage to farms there that had loans from the Federal Land Bank in Baltimore. He was in Porto Rico for about a week before returning. When he came home after that trip, he brought souvenirs to us and movie films he had taken. The trip was a first for him to a foreign place and also on an Ocean Liner. His first attempt at making movies was not very good, but we enjoyed his telling us about the different seances.

At Thanksgiving that year Daddy told us that after Christmas we would leave the farm and move to Baltimore to live with him. He said that we would live in the same apartment building he was living in, but two apartments on the 6th floor would be combined to make enough room for us. He said that Paul and I would go to an elementary public school four blocks from the apartment and Katie would go to a high school.

The last class before Christmas vacation, Miss White gave a transfer note to me to give to my new school. I said, "Goodbye" to my classmates and bus companions. We did not take any furniture as the apartment was already furnished, but all of our clothes were packed into our car along with us. It was a long ride on two-lane roads and through small and large towns with numerous stop lights. We stopped at a filling station for gas, use the toilet and to eat the lunch that Mother had packed.

The three of us in the back seat traded places when we started again. It was a miserable trip that we were encouraged to make interesting by scenery, and by playing travel games. Daddy read the Burma Shave signs to us, and we would see who had the most white horses on her/his side of the road between towns. Going through Washington we went over the Potomac River bridge and right by the Capitol building. We were admonished to stop our bickering so Daddy could concentrate on driving.

Arriving in Baltimore was still a long drive through streets with buildings packed close together and lots of cross streets with stop lights before we got to the Bradford Apartment building at the corner of Saint Paul and 33rd street. It was late in the day when we five cramped and tired people got out of the car. Daddy parked in back and had help unloading our things and taking them up the elevator to our 6th floor apartment. Mother and Daddy had a room with a pull-down Murphy double bed, Paul and I had a room with two single beds, and Katie had a separate room. There was a dining room, a small kitchen and two bathrooms. Our windows faced the back and side of the building so we could not see traffic on the streets below.

Daddy took Katie to enroll in an all-girls public high school, but when they got there he saw that most of the students were either Jews or dark-skinned foreign-looking girls. He did not enroll her and later enrolled her in a private high school.

Daddy walked with Paul and me to our first day of school at Margaret Brent Elementary on St. Paul and 29th Street. It was four long city blocks straight down St. Paul and on the way to the Federal Land Bank on 24th Street. The school was a two-story red-brick building with a high chain-link fence around an asphalt-surface play area on one side and against the side walk. Daddy went in with us and registered us as new pupils.

I was already in displacement shock, and this school took me into academic and culture shock too. The teacher and children were speaking an unintelligible language with a mouthful of mush, and the pupils already knew the multiplication tables. At the end of school that day, Paul and I walked home together. During the next days, weeks and months I learned the new language fairly well, and I recognized the buildings and street signs to and from school, but I had a really hard time with the class lessons. Two new subjects for me were once-a-week music and art. Our music teacher played a violin, and she coached us in singing. The popular song, Deep Purple, was on her "must do" agenda. I could not carry a tune, so after failing an embarrassing trial as a soloist I just needed to learn the lyrics. I did that part OK and remembered them long enough to get passing grades in music.

I was an outsider at school, and living on the 6th floor of an apartment house did not include any neighbors with children. When we got home from school Mercer, the elevator operator, would take us up to our floor. Most good-weather days we would get our roller skates and balls and go back down to the next door large vacant lot and long concrete walk along the street up a sloping hill. Sometimes before it was time to go in for supper, one of us had to use the toilet. Mercer never said anything, but he did not always seem especially happy either.

I was really homesick and missed the children in school at Climax, especially Jewel. I found a stamped post card in the writing desk

95

and wrote a note to her and put it in the mail box in the apartment lobby. I put my address on it and hoped she would write back. About a week later when Daddy got home from work Mother gave him a letter that had come. A short time afterward, he had the opened letter and said he needed to talk with me in my room. He sat in a chair and I sat on my bed. He took the letter and a pieced-together post card from the envelope. He read the letter from Jewel's mother. It went like this: *Dear Mr. Crider, my daughter, Jewel, received this post card from your son, Walter. When she took it from the mail box, she tore it up. I made her paste it back together, and when I read it, I gave her a switching, and I expect you to do the same to your son. Mrs. Fox.* I saw the post card that had been torn into small pieces and pasted back together. I don't think Daddy read it to me, but I knew what I had written which went something like this: *Dear Jewel, I am doing alright, but I sure do miss you. I love you and wonder if you will give me a piece of pu**y? Love, Walter.* Daddy had a hair brush in his hand, and started talking to me. He said that I should not write such things on a post card where every body could read it and that I should never do such a thing again. In an attempted defense, I said that I meant after we were grown up. I don't think he replied to that, but said that he needed to do what Jewel's mother requested and for me to pull my pants down and bend across his lap. He gave me several hard swats with the back of the hair brush on my bare bottom and left me in my room until supper time.

That was the only instruction Daddy ever gave me on sex, and we never had any other conversation about it either. Daddy never said anything about it again. Mother never said anything, and I did not tell anyone, but I was ashamed, sorry, embarrassed and very sure that I had ruined any chance I could possibly have with Jewel. I was sad and worried for a long time that Paul would find out and tease me forever by threatening to tell other people.

About Easter Mother got infections in mastoid bones behind both of her ears. We were told that she was in a very serious condition. Lou came from Norfolk to look after us while Mother was in the hospital in the next block from us on 33rd Street. Mother came home after 3 or 4 days, and Lou staid a few more days until she recovered enough to take care of us. I think Katie helped a lot too.

A drainage opening had been left behind each of Mother's ears, and a gauze tape had been packed in to absorb fluids and help healing where part of the mastoid bone had been removed. Dr, Cannon came every few days to replace the gauze. I was curious and watched him several times when he came. About the time Mothers surgery had healed, I got a severe ache in my left ear. Dr. Cannon came and found I had an infection in my inner ear. He gave me some medication and ordered bed rest. I was no better the next day, and my temperature was well above normal. Dr. Cannon came and used a pointed small scalpel to puncture my ear drum and drain the fluid from my inner ear. I continued taking pills and staying in bed as Dr. Cannon came each day to monitor my condition. My temperature gradually returned to normal, and the ear drum healed. I guess being in bed so long with a fever had weakened me so that I developed bronchial pneumonia. Dr. Cannon treated me for that as I continued staying at home. By the time I was well enough to return to school, there were only a couple of school weeks left. Mother and Daddy

(I think mostly Mother) decided that it was better that I not return and made arrangements with my teachers and principal to give me an incomplete grade for my fourth grade attendance. When the two weeks were up, Mother was packed and more than ready to leave Baltimore for Windcrest. I don't know how Daddy felt, but we three children were ready too!

The preacher at Greenpond, Mr. Kessler, had been replaced by Mr. W. L. Naff. He was about middle aged and did not have children living with him and his wife. His preaching manner was almost opposite to that of Mr. Kessler. His voice was gentle and not energetic. His message was persuading instead of accusing, and his sermon subjects were kind and promising rather than vicious and threatening. At summer revival I answered his call to repent of my sins and to ask for forgiveness by walking down the aisle and becoming a church member. When the invitational hymn was over, church members came to congratulate me and to welcome me into the church. On the way home, Mother said she was proud of me.

Baptismal services were a Sunday or two later at Anderson's Mill. We converts were dressed in white. The girls wore white dresses, and the boys wore white shirts and white duck long trousers. All of us wore tennis shoes. Mr. Naff wore a black suit and tie and a white shirt. The choir sat on towels or mats on the bank overlooking the head race. Cousin Otey would periodically let water out of the raceway to adjust the water level to suit the height of the convert. There were six or seven of us converts on the opposite side of the race from the choir. The choir sang without any musical instruments, and started their series of hymns a little before the baptisms started.

Mr. Naff called to the assembled to bow their heads, and he said a prayer thanking "Our Almighty God" for bringing these repentant souls into the heavenly joy of salvation. He then waded into the waist-high water and took the hand of the first person to help him into the race. With a handkerchief in his left hand held over the person's mouth and nose and his right arm holding his waist behind, he said, "In the name of Jesus Christ I now baptize you into His Heavenly Kingdom" and pushed the person backwards to immerse him briefly before bringing him upright. A church member on the bank had a towel to dry the emerging new member. This ritual was repeated until all converts had been baptized. All new members were welcomed by the choir and other church members. I think this started my lasting subliminal feeling of guilt by knowing I could never live the life that God demanded.

Our cow, Buttercup, came in heat, and the nearest Guernsey bull was about a mile away and owned by Mr. Tom Bailey. Mother gave Paul a dollar and told him and me to take Buttercup there and have her serviced by Mr. Bailey's bull. Paul held the halter rope and walked in front. I was the tail-twister and walked in back with a switch to make her go when she stopped. Mr. Bailey was at his house near the road, and when Paul told him what we wanted, we walked to his stable where he called his bull which was some distance away in his pasture. The bull answered with a bellow, and we could hear him coming at a run. He was all business and started smelling and licking Buttercup's genital before then rearing to her back and unsheathing a long red rigid penis with a hook-shaped end and shoving it into her genital with a jumping hunch and then dismounting. Buttercup had just stood still and did not do anything. His penis was limp, and he stood there while Buttercup tried to turn her head and lick him. Mr. Bailey said that to make sure she was bred that we should wait to let him go another time. In a little while, the bull with stiff penis again went to Buttercup again. Paul paid Mr. Bailey who fastened his bull in a stall, and Paul, Buttercup and I started home. I had watched transformed in amazement and thinking, "So this is how you do it. Wow!"

Mother talked with Uncle Fletcher about my making up my incomplete fourth grade by getting tutored during the summer. It was decided that Cousin Maude's oldest daughter, Mary, who was an elementary school teacher was qualified and willing to teach me to meet the passing requirements of fourth grade. I was still ashamed for having wet Cousin Maude's bed, but they were nice enough to not say anything about it. I went to Miss Easley's house about a mile from our house three mornings each week for my lessons. Sometimes mother took me, sometimes I would walk and sometimes I rode Katie's Shetland pony, Brownie. Except when it was raining or I rode Brownie, I usually walked home at lunch time. Because I was the only pupil, Miss Easley gave me a lot of help and quizzed me often to reinforce her lessons. Her daddy, Cousin Charlie, enjoyed asking me questions about my studies and especially about the multiplication tables. He laughed at all my wrong answers. After about two months, Miss Easley sent in the certificate verifying that I had met the requirements to pass the fourth grade.

Later that summer, Mother said that we were going to live in our house in Chatham for the next school year. Uncle Doug would move all of our furniture, but Paul and I would lead Buttercup along the road. Before the last load of furniture had been loaded on the truck, Paul, Buttercup and I started on the 12-mile journey. Paul was the leader, and I was the tail twister and switcher to help Buttercup's incentive to keep walking. Every now and then she would stop. Paul would pull on the rope and shout at me to make her go. I would twist her tail until it hurt her, and I would use the switch too. It was a long walk, and the three of us were tired by the time we had gone half way. When we reached Floyd Fox's filling station about 3/4th of the way to Chatham, Uncle Doug's truck came up the road from the direction of Chatham again and went on by us. This time the driver only went a little ways to where he could turn around and came back and stopped. He helped Paul and me get Buttercup up the lowered tail gate an tie her in the truck. Paul and I rode beside the driver to our house where he unloaded Buttercup at the stable. What a relief to get there.

Paul and I shared one room upstairs and Katie had the other, and there was one bathroom. Down stairs there was a central hall with stairs; a parlor with fireplace, dining room and kitchen on one side and a living room, bed room, bath room and back porch on the other. Mother and Daddy slept downstairs. There was a porch across the front. We were across the street and one door down from the elementary school. Katie went to Chatham High School near downtown.

My fifth grade teacher was Miss Maggie East. I did not know any of the pupils in my class. Miss East was a small lady and a strict teacher who demanded good conduct. I think I did well enough to continue getting my usual C and D grades, and I made friends with some of my classmates during recess. One of my punishments was a homework assignment to write 100 times, "I will not talk in class." I don't remember much about the lessons we were taught that year, just that I passed.

Jim Davis collected stamps and I became interested in his collection and learned about how to do it. After I started, we would trade some of our duplicate stamps that the other did not have. We bought stamps by mail, and we searched through old letters at home. Marse Ferrell lived a couple of miles from Chatham and rode the school bus. Charles Mundy and Buddy Overby were other boys I played with. One day in class a girl passed a note with my name on it to me. I opened the folded paper and was reading it when Miss East called out to me to come to the front of the class and read the note out loud. *"Dear Water do you like me or Boots best? Eunice Guyer."* I could feel a hot red flash and sweat over my whole body, and I could not see or hear anything except the way back to my desk where I went and tried to become invisible. When school was out for the day, it seemed like every one in school had learned about the note and started, "Hey *Water* do you like me best?" I just hung my head and walked home as fast as I could. I don't know how Eunice and Boots Eanes felt, and I wasn't thinking about asking.

The other girls that I remember in my class were Anise Davis, Charlotte Meadows, Annie Laurie Mundy and Lois Bennett. Charles' and Annie Laurie's Daddys were brothers and had a grocery store in town. They lived in the Woodlawn suburb of Chatham.

Paul was in seventh grade at Chatham Elementary and one of his teachers was Mr. Hooker who was also the Principal. His other teacher was Miss Shelton who boarded in Uncle Joe's house on Main Street. Paul and I never walked to school together, and had no contact at School. He played baseball with some classmates at recess. His friends were Allen Davis (Anise's brother), Vernon Guyer (Eunice's brother), Jim Pickle, a Earls boy and some more. One girl in his class, Lucy Jim Davis (Jim Davis's sister). She was the prettiest girl I had ever seen (including Jewel Fox), and Paul was one of her ardent admirers.   Paul and I were in separate groups at school except when I got the note from Eunice. He was in the group after school who was teasing and jeering me.

At the end of the school year, Miss Shelton climbed out of her first-floor window into the arms of Uncle Joe's son, John, and the two eloped into marriage.

When the movie, "Sleeping Beauty", came to Chatham, Mother took us to see it. We got to the movie theater early and were waiting for the ticket booth and doors to open when Mrs. Fox, Lucile and Jewel came. Panic almost overtook me. I hung back and was waiting for some big argument to start between Mrs. Fox and Mother. I don't know what was said, but they started talking and smiling. Lucile was Paul's age, and they knew each other and spoke a few words. I only looked at Jewel through the corner of my eye, and she seemed happy and not upset to see me. I just wanted to get away and was glad when the ticket booth and doors opened. It also was a relief that Mother did not have us sit next to them. I was nervous during the whole movie and really glad that Mother did not linger to talk after the movie.

Uncle Hurt's oldest child, Richard Harrison Whitehead was living in Arizona on a ranch that he had obtained through homesteading. When he was 17 he joined the army to fight in the World War and was sent to

Europe where he suffered a chemical gas attack that damaged his lungs. When he came home, the moist air in Chatham intensified his breathing difficulty. He and his sister, Elizabeth, decided to homestead joining tracts in the dry western part of Arizona. This would get relief for Richard and furnish a better chance of ranching success with a larger ranch. Richard drove home in a two-seat Model A ford that had a fold-down top and rain curtains. Elizabeth had stayed on their ranch near Kirkland, but Richard brought his police dog, Rex, which was protection for him at night when he slept in the car. Rex's daddy was Rin Tin Tin, Tom Mix's movie dog. We had seen movies starring Tom Mix and his companion dog and were really excited to see Rex. Richard said that we should not play with him because he was a guard dog for his angora goats and he might bite us. That gave us a lot of respect and long-distance admiration for Rex. Richard wore western boots and clothes, and he wore a western hat made of some kind of gray fur. He was not a big person, but he was a real COWBOY! And the only one we had ever seen and actually talked to.

Another cousin who had left Chatham for employment was Uncle Walter's oldest child, Walter Hurt (nick name "Chunk".) He worked for the American Tobacco Company who sent him to China to buy tobacco. After a couple or three years, he came home with stories of his experience in a very foreign country. He also brought souvenirs that I did not see, but he gave a few strange-looking coins to some of the older children that I did see. He stayed at home and worked in Uncle Walter's grocery and general store.

Sometimes Mother would send me up town to buy groceries at

Uncle Walter's general merchandise and grocery store. One time in early December while I was in the store, a colored man asked for "Nigger Toes". Uncle Walter waited on him and weighed out the amount of nuts he wanted. I had been told the name of these long, black, hard-shelled triangular nuts was "Nigger Toes", but I was surprised that a colored man would call them by that name. I guess he was like me and didn't know them by any other name. When I got home, I told Mother about the nut sale and my surprise. She said that the real name was Brazil Nuts, but everybody called them Nigger Toes. I think I started calling them Brazil Nuts after that.

Another time I went to town on an errand for Mother was to get her "biscuit beater" repaired. One of the foods that she was proud of and always served on special occasions was her beaten biscuits. For her to make them, she needed a biscuit block and a dough beater. The biscuit block was an 18'-inch long section of a 2-ft.-diameter tree trunk with three 2-ft.-long legs in one end. The beater was a round iron rod about 2ft. long attached to a 1in.-square bar about 4in. Long. Periodically the bar would break loose from the handle. There was a blacksmith shop in town next to the Moeshler builder's supply store. I don't remember the blacksmith's name, but in addition to a forge it had a wood lathe and other tools. He made and repaired wagons and wagon wheels and put new iron parts on wagons, plows and farm tools. I was interested in the different things he had and especially his use of his Model T Ford to turn the lathe. He had two 6-inch diameter iron pipes lying close to each other in a wood trough about 10 ft. long. The pipes had bearings on each end, and a little from one end was a flat belt that went around one pipe and up around a pulley on a shaft near the ceiling. On the other end of the shaft was another pulley with a belt running down to his lathe that was mounted on a bench. To use the lathe, he would back the back wheels onto the pipes, put the car in gear to turn the back wheels and adjust the speed to turn the lathe. He could leave the car running and use belt tighteners to start and stop the lathe.

He let me turn the forge blower to heat the two pieces of the biscuit beater until they were hot enough for him to weld them together by beating the over-lapping pieces with a heavy hammer against his anvil while tuning them to keep the mended handle straight. I was sorry when he had Mother's biscuit beater repaired.

Shortly after she had left Larry and gone to Norfolk, Sallie came back to her teaching job and went back to live with Larry. Now she had come home again to have a baby and also to separate from Larry again. She wasn't at home long before she went to the hospital in Danville and had a baby boy March 4, 1935, Paul Booker, named for his two grandfathers. I was sick and had stayed home from school the day Larry came and rang the door bell. Mother saw who it was through the door glass and told me to lie down on the love seat in the living room and to not leave as long as Larry was there. Larry said that he had come to see his son and Sallie. Mother told him to wait in the living room while she got Sallie, and said that I was sick and home from school. I think we spoke to each other, and soon Sallie came with Paul Booker. They sat on the sofa and talked in a low voice for awhile. Then Larry said that maybe I should go to my room. Sallie did not say anything, and I said that Mother told me to stay there on the love seat. He did not say any more to me, and after a short time he left.

Sallie decided to get a divorce from Larry, but she found out that was not easy to do in Virginia. Marse Ferrell's mother, Marguerite, had gone to Reno, Nevada where after a six-week residency, she was granted a divorce. Mother talked to Uncle Joe who was the county Commonwealth Attorney. He said that he could not accept private legal cases, but would have some other lawyer in town handle Sallie's petition. Sallie and Paul Booker continued living with us until her divorce was granted, and she continued staying with us until she started teaching that fall at Renan Elementary School.

She found a boarding house with Mr. and Mrs Parker on the Renan school-bus route. It was across the road from Straight Stone Baptist Church, and Mrs. Parker would also care for baby Paul. The Parkers were also keeping their grandson, Arthur Ryan, Jr. who was a sophomore at Renan.

Mother and Daddy decided that we would go back to the farm for the summer, and that Uncle Doug would move all of our possessions, including Buttercup. All three of we children were glad to be going back HOME , and especially Paul and I that Uncle Doug would be hauling Buttercup.

Chapter 7

Hargrave and Farming

Another Mixture

Our new sharecropper, Bus Nibblet, had a daughter, Mae Nanny, who was about 16 and had a baby, Odessa, living with him and the rest of his family. Mother wanted household help and hired Mae Nanny who was taught to do the work and to cook the way mother wanted. She was a quick learner and soon gave Mother more time to spend with us. Usually Mae Nanny came early to help with breakfast and stayed until after dinner before going home, so I did not see her much during school days.

I was in the kitchen when she and Mother were talking about how she came to have Odessa. She said that she had gone to their mail box and was going back home when a cousin took her into a barn and did it to her. She did not say who the cousin was but went on to say that when Odessa started coming it felt like she was going to the bathroom and did not hurt much. Mother and Mae Nanny sort of looked at me during the conversation and did not say any more about Odessa.

Another incident I remember about the Nibblets involved Paul and Junior who was just a little older and bigger than Paul. Paul, Bus and I were on the wagon with Junior driving the pair of mules to get sand from the creek on the lower place. Junior wanted the mules to go faster and started whipping them with the free end of the leather reins. Paul told him to stop whipping the mules, but Junior said that he was driving and would do what he wanted. Paul then tussled with Junior and took the reins. They hit each other a few times and Paul had a bruise and scratches. I think Junior kept driving, but he quit whipping the mules. We loaded sand from along the creek bank and returned home. When Mother asked what happened. Paul told her of the incident with Junior. Mother became very upset, and went outside where Uncle Bus was helping Junior spread the sand in our driveway. Mother, who had always been very helpful and polite to every colored person I had seen her with, became a stranger to me. She was vigorously angry and shouting threatening things at Uncle Bus. If ever any of his family fought with her children again, he would be gone from her farm, and she would have the sheriff arrest him. Uncle Bus hung his head and said in a low voice that he would settle with Junior. Mother came back into the house still fuming.

I don't think we had much contact with the Nibblet children until tobacco harvest. Junior had a younger brother and two sisters younger than he was. All of them helped. Uncle Bus and Junior pulled the ripe leaves and put them into a narrow sled with 3-ft.-high sides of burlap bags pulled by a mule between the rows. When a sled was full, Junior drove the mule to the shade of some Oak trees near a curing barn. He unhooked the mule, hooked him to an empty sled and went back to the field for more. His brother and sisters, and sometimes Paul and I would use cotton twine to make a loop around the stems of small bunches of leaves and rotate alternate bunches to fall on the opposite side of the stick. When the stick was full, the twine was tied and broken, and that full stick was layed in a pack on a wagon. The next stick would be placed on the tying stand, twine tied on one end and bunches of leaves that his sisters had arranged by their stems into neat bunches to repeat the process. I handed leaves and watched them being tied. I then would tie some, but I was not as fast as the boy and soon went back to handing leaves.

That fall of 1935 my 6th grade teacher at Climax was Miss Elizabeth Motley. This was her first year of teaching, and because she was so smart she skipped a grade in school and was just 18 years old. For our Health class, we had Miss Collins while Miss Motley taught high school freshman English. Jewel Fox was in the class, I was really glad she was, but I still felt ashamed and very shy around her. A second cousin, Helen Blair, was in my class too and a distant cousin Dorothy Walker. Jewel was friends with Louise and Virginia Bennett, and I talked with them some. I had not told anyone about my post card, but I did not know if Jewel had. I was nervous for a long time after school started, but I was friends with several boys. One of them was Junior Smith and another was a distant cousin, Taz Anderson. Miss Motley was a friendly and a very good teacher, and she had good discipline without being overly strict. One of the boys put a small mirror on his shoe and tried to look up Miss Motley's dress when she stopped to check the work of a student in the next row. I don't know if he ever saw anything, but he said he did. He never got caught. I made better grades that year, and I think I learned more too.

Paul was a freshman in high school and played on the baseball and basketball teams. In addition to regular academic subjects, he took Agriculture and was a member of the FFA. He had to have a project and chose raising chickens. His hen hatched some eggs and the little chicks had grown normally up to feathering when he could tell that about half were males and the other half were females. His teacher, Mr. Gordon Trent, came after school one day to show him how to make capons from the roosters by removing the gonads from inside the abdomen. Someway

Paul held the first young rooster while Mr. Trent made a small cut in the rooster's lower abdomen, then with a button-hook-like instrument pushed the hook end through the incision and pulled out a pinkish cord with a swollen place in it. He said that was one of the gonads. He then cut on each end of the gonad and let it fall to the ground. He then repeated the process to pull out and remove the second. The new capon was turned loose, and he held the next rooster for Paul. With continuing instructions, Paul followed the procedure and removed the two gonads. I watched intently.

Mother needed to have medical surgery of some kind, and she wanted to have it done in the same hospital in Baltimore where her mastoid surgery was done. She asked her sister, Aunt Katie Watson to look after us. The principal at Climax was Mr. George Jones who lived in Chatham. Aunt Katie agreed to keep us, and Uncle Fletcher requested Mr. Jones to take us to school and back each day with him in his convertible. When we got to school the first day in Mr. Jones' car, the other children wondered why we were brought to school in the principal's car. They thought we were his special favorites, but Mr. Jones did not seem happy with his assignment. Another nervous situation for me, and another failure for both Paul and me. When we got home from school, our wet sheets had been washed and were hanging over her stair banisters and railings to dry. Aunt Katie did not say anything about the wet beds. I wanted to go somewhere and just live by myself.

That Christmas my special gift was a telescope and a pair of leather knee-high lace-up boots with a snap-flap pocket knife pouch. They were just what I wanted to check my rabbit traps. I could walk in rain or snow to where I could see the trap then use my telescope to get a closer view to see if the trap door was still up or was down and know if I needed to walk any farther.

Paul got a single-shot, bolt-action 22 rifle and some bullets. Daddy gave him some safety instructions. Paul already knew how to load and shoot it. Daddy and Paul practiced shooting at targets in the front yard away from the stable and chicken house. I watched and was allowed to shoot it. I loaded it after my first shot and was deciding on my next target when it went off. My heart skipped a beat or two until I saw no one was hit. The rifle had been pointing up away from anything or anyone. That was a lasting lesson to me about gun safety.

That fall of 1936, Daddy wanted Mother to go back to Baltimore with him. We three children were part of the discussion and were asked if we wanted to go back. I was going to be in the seventh grade, Paul would be a sophomore in high school and Katie would be a senior. None of us wanted to go. Our other choice was for Paul and me to go to Hargrave and Katie to go to Averett Junior College and advanced high school. We decided to go to the boarding schools.

Mother took Paul and me to Hargrave where we had already had our tuition and fees paid. We each were assigned a room and given uniforms to fit. Paul's room was on Floyd Hall in the high school building and mine was in the Junior Building. Mrs. Crews was the House Mother for us elementary school children. She mended clothes, sewed on buttons, gave special attention to homesick children and in general served as a surrogate mother. All of our classes were in the Junior Building, and we marched as "C Company" to our meals in the main building mess hall.

We had about 30 junior students grades 4 to 7 living on the two floors. My teachers in the 7th grade were Mrs. Tune who was the wife of the high school math teacher, Major Tune, and Mrs. Brooks, the wife of the higher math and Latin teacher, Captain Brooks. There were no girls enrolled at Hargrave, and both teachers were caring and effective teachers.

My room had a double-deck bunk bed, a closet, two small desks and a dresser with mirror. I do not remember the name of my roommate who had the upper bunk. My first night was a horrible experience of worry. I planned, but at the same time tried to not think of the consequences of wetting my bed. However, it did happen. Not only the sheet, but the mattress was also wet. We had been taught how to make our beds with a four-point tucked-in blanket. At the head of the bed the top sheet and blanket was to be folded back about a foot and the sides tucked in leaving space for the pillow to be neatly in place. I had been partly successful with only a small wet place by going to the toilet as late as I could stay awake. So I made my bed as though nothing had happened. Only my roommate knew, but his bed was much wetter than mine. He had no chance to hide his. At bed check, Mrs. Crews was notified and furnished a dry mattress, a rubber under-sheet and clean sheets for him. She must have checked my bed too, because she did the same for me. My bed-wetting problem after that first time, became very seldom and finally was cured. I guess the fear of humiliation had more effect than all the medicinal treatments I had tried.

Learning to be a soldier was a large part of being a cadet. Bugle calls from reveille to taps signaled our military instructions. Each call was unique and signaled a required action to be taken. Our three meals in the mess hall required us to line up in formation outside the Junior Building and march to the mess hall where we had been assigned tables and chairs. A faculty member was the head at each of our tables. The food followed a scheduled menu for the 21 meals each week. It was not home cooking, and for my first time, there were no choices. I either ate what was served or went hungry with hope the next meal would be more to my liking. I learned to choke down some foods that I did not like. Some of them became more edible, and some I learned to actually like.

If the weather was suitable, after classes we would assemble as our Company of two platoons in lines of squads and march to a level field behind the Junior Building. There we were taught to walk in step, right and left face, about face and do the marching movements of column right and column left. Another part of our marching activities required properly carrying and handling a wooden rifle replica. One of these was assigned to each junior cadet and was required to be polished and handled in a professional manner. Each weighed about 5-7 pounds which was not too heavy for the younger fourth grade students. Saturday morning after breakfast and before lunch was for room inspections.

The cadet in military charge of the Junior school was a high school Captain senior who shared a room on the first floor with a senior-school sergeant junior. The two of them would inspect each cadet's room for cleanliness and order. Demerits were given for any deficiencies. Accumulated demerits would deprive the recipient of some privilege or require some mild punishment. Saturday afternoon was free time when we could go into Chatham to get a haircut or go to a movie. The movie was nearly always a western and included a segment of a serial that was continued with the next segment on the following weekend. Sunday mornings were for marching to a church of your choice or a bus ride to Danville for Catholics and for a parade in the late afternoon. One Sunday, Aunt Katie had me for a big dinner with her family. Her house was close to the Hargrave campus through a short-cut path between them. I staid longer than I should have to get back before the parade, but I made it on time. With my full stomach using up a lot of digestive blood, standing at attention during the ceremony caused me to faint and fall. A couple of cadets pulled me to the back of our formation and left me to recover while they returned to formation.

The military faculty Commandant, Lieutenant Gordon Judd, was detailed from the US Army and commanded all military activities. I did not have much contact with him except during parades when we marched past him in review. A very emotional experience for me was when a cadet was found guilty of stealing another cadet's property and sentenced to be expelled. For this ceremony, all cadets were lined on each side of the long concrete walk from the front of the senior building to the "Hargrave Arch" on Military Drive. A description of his crime and of his punishment was read on the front steps by Lt. Judd. Then with rolling of drums, a cadet officer on each side of the offender took their places, and the drummers formed two lines behind them. The drummers provided cadence as the expelled cadet was escorted along the walk lined by us cadets on each side. Waiting at the arch was a car which took him and the escorting officers to the train station where he was put on the train to his home town. He had been "Drummed out of the Corps." Sadness, anger and a few indescribable emotions depressed me for a long time because of his public shaming.

About the last couple of months before school was out, Mrs. Tune was going to have a baby and quit teaching. Her replacement was Spr the brother-in-law of the school's Headmaster and President, Colonel Aubrey H. Camden. Major Sprat had shiny black "patent leather-like" hair brushed back with no part, yellow stains on his fingers from cigarette smoke, wore very neat and fashionable clothes and the only man I had known who wore white or tan spats over highly-polished black shoes. In addition to these physical appearances, he had a moderately deep voice. His teaching skills were not up to Mrs. Tunes, but his more relaxed manner and his selection of English literature was admired by me. Each afternoon for the last lesson of the day, he read part of an Arthur Conan Doyle's *Sherlock Holmes* story. In my mind and imagination, he was Sherlock.

In early May of 1937 there was a lot of excited interest in the Hindenburg Zeppelin fire and disaster in New Jersey. The radio reports were by excited and astounded reporters describing the real-time tragic events of passengers with clothes on fire jumping from the hydrogen-burning airship that was still nearly a hundred feet in the air. The fast Atlantic Ocean crossing by an airship had been anticipated with great expectations of an air-travel wonderland future.

Summer on the farm was a lot of work and play. Paul milked the two cows, buttercup and Cherry, twice each day. I fed chickens and cleaned the chicken houses. We both worked in the vegetable garden, helped get up hay and harvest and thresh wheat.

Clyde had decided to go and farm with Mazie's father, Mr.

Bradner, so Daddy hired Andrew Hubbard who had helped dig our well.

The Nibblets had moved to sharecrop on another farm, so Mother was looking for a cook to replace May Nannie. Raleigh Bowen was about 15 and looking for work. He asked Mother if he could get the job. He did and learned to cook the way Mother wanted. He also brought in wood for the kitchen stove and helped with the garden vegetables, especially in canning them.

This is when I started learning more about Raleigh as a person instead of as a playmate and teacher. Raleigh took his job seriously and was a quick learner. Word got around the community and to Raleigh's boy relatives and friends that Raleigh had taken a "woman's' job as a cook. Did not take long for boys riding on wagons going along the road taking wheat and corn to Anderson Mill for grinding that they looked for Raleigh picking vegetables in our roadside garden. They had a hilarious time jeering and "funning" him. "Hey cook, what are we having for dinner?" was one of the phrases shouted at him. Raleigh laughed with them, and gave them a menu and asked if they wanted some. No shame or intimidation, but enjoying his job and the money he was making. I'm not sure, but I think he included with a little pride in his response, "I have a job."

Raleigh's job continued on through the late winter, spring and summer. Paul and I were especially glad to have Raleigh as cook. In addition to being a good cook and a lot of help to mother he did some of the chores that we had been doing. Raleigh had not gone to school, and now he really wanted to learn how to read, write and do numbers. He saved his money and bought clothes and shoes so he could start school in the fall.

In addition to accepting the intended shame and ridicule of being a "cook", he took an even more "unusual" position that invited more hilarious ridicule. He was going to school!!!

As they say, "Saying you are going to do something and actually doing it are two different things." Also, "The proof is in the pudding." From the day Raleigh made public that he intended going to school, he received skepticism and a lot of advice. Especially from his family who did not want him to waste his time and money. He also reinforced his determination and courage. Not he kind of courage mustered in the heat of an emotional atmosphere in an encounter with violent consequences. There are a lot of reports of the latter kind. War; robberies; gang fights; physical violence of all kinds. Raleigh had the cold-bloodied courage to do what he believed in. To willfully expose himself as a person to what ever may come. With determination, forethought and a dream, he started the first step by buying new clothes. Never too late to back out and save his "normal" self. The first step did not seem to make the second any easier. Putting his foot on the step of the school bus and entering for the ride to school. He, a 15-year-old young man entered Mrs. Reynolds' first grade classroom and asked to be enrolled. Mrs. Reynolds was a mature lady who had taught first grade at Climax for many years and had developed a kindly and caring personality to help frightened little children to adjust to being away from home and in a strange place with strangers. She gave   Raleigh a little relief from his stress when she welcomed him and immediately had a larger desk and chair moved in for him. She inquired about his previous school experience to determine where to get him started in his studies. Pretty much zero for Raleigh, so his education started at the same level as the rest of the children in his class.

Paul and I were cutting grass in the front yard when some Gibson boys were across the road on their way to visit the the Bowens. They had a switch and were beating and kicking their hound dog trying to make him stop following them and go back home. The dog came over into our driveway where Paul was working, and Paul went to the dog to pet it after the beating. However, the dog must have thought Paul's outstretched arm was going to be another blow and jumped up with his front paws on Paul's shoulders and bit his nose. Paul yelled and the dog ran away leaving blood running from Paul's nose. Some way the Gibson boys and dog were gone. Mother washed his face and put iodine and a bandage on the gash near the end of his nose. She called Dr. Parrish who came and put a few stitches to hold the cut together and redressed the wound. He asked if the dog had been vaccinated for rabies, and if not would the owner agree to have the dog killed and tested. We did not know, but after Mother talked to the father of the boys, Mr. Jerry Gibson, found that the dog had not been vaccinated, and he would not agree to have his dog killed.

When Dr. Parrish was told of the situation with Mr. Gibson, he said that to be safe from rabies Paul would need to take a series of four injections into his abdomen. He came that afternoon for the first inoculation. Dr. Parrish and Paul went into our parlor. I couldn't see or hear anything until Paul started yelling, "ow, ow, ow", and Dr. Parrish said, "Hold still." When the yelling and talking stopped, Dr. Parrish then said, "Boy, you have skin as tough as a mule's hide." Dr. Parrish left and said that he would be back in three days for the second dose. Dr. Parrish came and gave Paul his second dose with the same yelling and admonishment as the first. He came two more times. The last was two weeks after the first. Those times were the few times I ever knew Paul to cry.

Dr. Parrish sterilized his instruments, needles and hypodermic syringes using the standard pressurized steam sterilizer. All were reused, and I think none of the needles were ever sharpened. Being stuck by one was painful to the extent of torture, and to be stuck in the abdomen was even worse. Dr. Parrish was not a skilled surgeon so Paul's nose gradually healed with a scar. It was not noticeable to most people except to him.

Andrew did the plowing in the garden, and he grew hay, corn and wheat on the farm. He could plow, harrow, plant and cultivate these crops, but at harvest time extra help was needed. Edward Moore was hired to help cut the wheat. Cutting wheat by hand with a cradle required that the wheat had to be mature with grains fully developed but not dry. Swinging the scythe cutting blade with six wood "fingers" spaced above it to catch the cut stalks would shatter grains from dry seed heads. After each cutting swing, Edward would hold the cradle handle with his right hand and use his left to grasp the stalks of wheat in the cradle's fingers and lay the "hand" on the ground behind him. It was always hot while doing this work because there could not be any dew left to cause molding of bound bundles. Swinging the cradle was hard work, and under hot sunshine made rest and water a frequent necessity. Edward used his "rest time" to sharpen the blade using a file or a rod-shaped sharpening stone. He wore a ragged straw hat, and he was always sweating. He had a pointed nose, and in spite of his frequent wiping, it constantly dripped sweat.

My dreaded job was to follow behind Edward, collect the hands of wheat and tie them into bundles. The stems were not dry and brittle, so a few stems were held together into a tying cord to bind the bundle into a "sheave". The wheat stubble and briers made the hot work even harder and slower for me. Andrew would collect the tied bundles and stack them into rain-resistant shocks to continue the drying process. Edward and Andrew would change jobs after each had cut a swath across the field and back.

Daddy had Andrew grow red clover for hay because of a high nitrogen nutrition. Andrew would mow the ripe clover riding a two-mule-drawn mower with a four-foot long cyclic cutting blade. Our land was not fertile enough to produce thick and tall hay, so the cut hay usually would dry enough to rake and put into the hay loft after a day or two of sun. We had a mule-drawn dump rake that Andrew would use to rake the hay into long windrows. Paul would rake some, but my legs were not long enough to reach the dump pedal. We had a hay frame with long poles as standards for the wagon. I usually stayed on the wagon to pack the loose hay Andrew and Paul would throw up using pitch forks. It was hard for me to keep from being buried under the hay until the wagon was moved to another place along the windrow. When the wagon was fully loaded, Andrew would climb up with me and drive the mules to the stable and stop under the loft door. The hay on the wagon was as high as the door, so

I could unlatch and open it and then step into the loft. Paul walked to the stable and came up the ladder to the loft where both of us would use pitch forks to move the hay back from the door where Andrew was throwing it. It was hot enough in the field, but nothing close to the heat under the tin roof of the hay loft. With no ventilation for the heat and dust, Paul's and my sweaty bare skin above and below our khaki shorts was caked with a layer of black paste. Between loads of hay, Paul and I would wash under the garden hose. Inside our noses was captured dust that took some blowing and wiping to get out.

After getting up hay, some evenings after supper when the humidity was high I would have a spell of asthma. The only relief we knew of was an injection of adrenaline that was required to be administered by a doctor. When my breathing became extremely difficult, Mother called Thelma at the switch board to be connected to cousin Dr. John Anderson, Jr. , who had replaced Dr. Parrish in Chatham. It was one of those still, quiet nights, and Dr. Anderson was a fast driver. It was not long before we could hear his car racing three miles away on the dirt road the other side of Climax. I could not breathe lying down, and he injected adrenaline into my upper leg muscle and waited for it to take effect. A couple of minutes later I was breathing normally, and my pulse rate was not elevated much. I was completely exhausted by the effort to breathe and fell asleep immediately after he left our bedroom.

Paul was always "in charge" and showed it by intimidating me and by his show of bravado. He could ride a bucking pony, milk cows, run the fastest and anything else he wanted to do to "show off." Threatening me seemed to me to be his biggest ego booster. One went too far when he was throwing rocks at me to make me run and jump. He said he did not mean to hit me, and I don't know if he did or not. I think he did not mean to hit me in the head because he could not throw accurately enough, but it did. I was knocked unconscious and had blood oozing from my hair. Paul was scared and helped me get to the house for mother to treat my wound. Mother used the usual stinging iodine and bandage, and to make sure I did not go into a coma she made sure I stayed awake and alert for a long time. Paul said it was an accident and he was sorry he hit me with the rock.

Late in June or early July, the shocks of wheat had become dry and ready to be stacked at a place for threshing. A wagon with a hay frame and standards was driven to each shock in the field where the sheaves were packed onto the wagon and hauled to a stack pole about 16 feet tall. Paul and I were too little to handle the sheaves. There were poles planted in the ground and boards lying on the ground around the stack pole. Sheaves with the grain end pointing toward the stack pole were placed around these poles in an inner and an outer circle to form the base of the stack. Progressive layers were added to a little more than 3/4ths up the pole where the two circles were gradually reduced to one and then to standing sheaves with the grain heads pointing down. We usually had three stacks of wheat.

Later, in July, Mr. Stowe in Dry Fork who had a threshing machine and a Fordson tractor would start threshing wheat for himself and for other farmers near him. At each farm he went to thresh, neighbors of that farmer would come to help and then he would go on to help those who had helped him. It was a revolving and changing group at each farm.

When threshing was being done close to us, Andrew was sent to help and would continue to help each farmer on the route to our farm and then continue to help those who helped us whose wheat had not yet been threshed.

It was a busy and hard day when the threshing machine came to our house. Mother and her new cook, Lena Fuller, did a lot of cooking. They had vegetables from our garden, sweet and butter milk, ice tea, fried chicken, pork chops, biscuits and corn bread and pies and cakes. Neighbor ladies came to help and brought food. Mr. Stowe set up his tractor with a long flat belt to a pulley on the thresher that was close to a stack of wheat. A man went up a homemade ladder to take the first sheaves from top and pitch them to a shelf on a platform at the front of the thresher. The man on the platform used a knife to cut the bound sheaf loose and feed the loose stalks head-first into the rotating and shaking thresher. Wheat grains were separated from the stems and surrounding chafe, sifted through screens that sent the straw out the back along with the grain sheaths (chafe) that were blown out with a fan. A constant supply of sheaves from the stack kept a constant flow of wheat, straw and chaff that had to be moved. Mr. Bowen had two metal half-bushel buckets that he alternately caught the wheat and poured it into burlap or cotton cloth bags. He used a note pad to keep a count of the number of buckets which he used to calculate the toll for Mr. Stowe. I don't know the percent he got.

Paul and I were not big enough to throw the straw for stacking around a poll or to pitch the sheaves to the machine feeders, so we got the only job we could do, and it was the worst one too. Pulling chafe from the back of the thresher. A lot of dust was blown out with the chaff, and it nearly choked us as it stuck all over us. Everyone was glad to hear the dinner bell, but none happier than me.

Wheat, straw and chaff were cleared from the machine before it was shut down. Everyone washed hands and face and went to the house to eat. The few colored men sat at a table on the back porch and the white men ate at our extended dining room table. A lot of food was eaten, and I did my part to help. Black and white men had the same kind and amount of food and were treated with the same social atmosphere, and the separation barrier was an accepted normal. As the deserts were eaten, compliments came from the men to Mother and the other women. They appreciated the verbal compliments, and seemed to enjoy even more talking about how much food and the way the men had enjoyed eating it.

Back to threshing the last stack of wheat and final clean up before the men left and Mr. Stowe got his tractor and threshing machine ready to move to the next farm. Paul and I washed up before a left-over supper and an early bed.

Chapter 8

Chickens, Pigg River and Baltimore

Foreign Country

Mother and Daddy had decided that Mother would remain at Windcrest for the 1936-37 school year. I would be a high school freshman at Climax and Paul would be a Junior. Katie would continue at Averett as a college freshman. I was glad to stay at home and not go back to Hargrave or Baltimore. It was like going home to be at a familiar school and with school friends. I think Miss Collins was my Homeroom and History teacher and the Agriculture teacher, Mr. Trent, was my science teacher. Miss Elizabeth Motley was the English teacher, and Miss Erma Bryant taught Algebra 1. I think that I made slightly better grades because I had been to Hargrave the previous year. Changing rooms between classes with different teachers and just being in high school gave some sense of pride to me. Mr. Hudson still drove the school bus, and Raleigh Bowen rode too. He had bought "proper" clothes for school and at age 15 enrolled in first grade. He took the teasing and kept going to school that year and two more years until he finished fourth grade when he could read and write at the level he wanted. I did not have the courage and determination that he had.

My classmates were mostly the same ones I had in other grades at Climax, so it was easy for me since I already had friends. The boys were big enough to play baseball and basketball as well as the usual marbles and jump rope. We mainly just talked with the girls except and occasional "tag" game with a girl you liked. Jewel seemed to still like me and would still talk to me, sometimes back and forth in class. Once in Algebra class when we were talking to each other, Miss Bryant became frustrated with us and sent us into the clothes closet and to shut the folding doors until we could get our talking over. I was really nervous. Jewel was not nervous at all. I hugged her, and she hugged back a little. We then decided to leave the closet, and the whole class started laughing and asking if we kissed. I was very excited and embarrassed, but I tried to act nonchalant and jokingly said, "I tried, but she bit me." Jewel laughingly replied, "I did not." We took our seats, and Miss Bryant almost got the class back to order before the bell.

Another similar experience happened in Science class when Mr. Trent sent Jewel and me outside into the hall. This time Jewel and I talked some in the hall just outside the classroom door. I told her I was sorry to get her in trouble, and she said that it was alright. At 14 I did not know what to do about my feelings for her. I think we sort of felt we were "*a pair*", but we couldn't actually do much about it except act sort of silly. She rode a different bus than I did, and she lived a long way on the other side of school from where I lived. It was too far away for me to walk.

When boys in my class got together, we talked about major league baseball and some other sports. Joe Louis was a sensational heavy-weight boxing champion, and he had frequent fights. We talked about the "Brown Bomber" and the boxers he knocked out. We also talked about Dizzy Dean, the St. Louis Cardinal pitcher. We also talked about the mysteries of girls. A couple of boys talked about having sex with a girl, but they did not give much detail. One boy a year older than me said he had found a rubber his daddy had used, and he washed it and used it himself.

At recess during the fall and spring, we played baseball. We had a bat carved from a hickory tree limb and a couple of balls made from tobacco tying twine wound tightly around a large marble or a little rubber ball until it was about the size of a regular baseball. We would choose sides to use the number of boys available to make up the teams. Junior Smith, "Smitty" threw left-handed and had a little movement on the balls he threw, so he usually was the pitcher on his team. I usually was the catcher on my team, and the rest of the players would take enough places to play. Sometimes we only had enough players to have one or two bases. Some of the other boys that played with us were Virgil Toney, Edgar Deboe and Jessie Watlington. We did not have a back stop, and I hated to miss a ball and have to run to get it.

Paul was on the regular high school baseball team. When we had home games with other high schools, they were in the afternoon after school was out. Paul and I would not ride the bus home and stay until the game was over. Two other boys on the Climax team that walked most of the way home with us were E. T. Atkins and his younger brother, Burman. They both were a little older than Paul.

When school was out that spring, Paul, Katie, Mother and I were back to a regular summer of work and play at Windcrest. I had used one of the two rooms of our double storage and feed building to raise chickens to frying size and sell them. I had a kerosene-burning brooder, mason-jar gravity waterers and metal trough-like feeders with wire guards to keep the little chicks out. Our Sears & Roebuck catalog listed baby chicks of several breeds that were delivered by mail. In the early spring, I ordered fifty of one of the "meat" breeds, and about a week later our mail carrier, Mr. Woodbridge, would bring my baby chicks to our mail box and blow his horn for us to come for my chicks.

The walls, floor and ceiling were covered with rat wire, but the wood floor over the wire was hard to keep clean. It would get wet and sticky from spilled water and chicken droppings. I had to work hard to keep the floor clean and keep water and feed for the chicks. The brooder had a hollow gas-filled disc that would expand and contract as the temperature changed and thus close or open a needle valve to control fuel flow to the brooder burner. Once the temperature was set to the proper warmth it staid very close to that setting. The little chicks would come from under the warm brooder hood to eat and drink and then go back as though they would with a mother hen. A few chicks died before they were large enough to discontinue using the brooder, and as they developed feathers I would move them outside into a wired-in lot with A-type small and movable houses until they were large enough to eat. This was a large part of my summer work.

I sold my frying-size chickens live to stores and relatives and friends in Chatham. The two stores at Climax that sold live chickens each bought a few, and Uncle Walter bought some at his store in Chatham. Uncle Walter, like the stores at Climax, kept his live chickens in cages in his store room at the back of his store and would kill them for the customers who bought them. After weighing the chicken for sale, he also would cut off the head and lower legs and clean out the entrails if the customer wanted him to. Aunt Katie and Aunt Elizabeth each would buy a few from me, and sometimes their neighbors would buy one or two. I made enough over my costs to have a little profit for my labor.

During the summer, Katie, Paul and I would visit back and forth with the Hudsons. We had bicycles and would ride about 5 miles on the dirt road to their house. I was always behind trying to keep up with Paul and Katie. We especially tried to sneak by the Tom Bailey house because his big hound would attack our pedaling feet and legs. He barked, snarled with bared teeth and tried to bite. We would try to keep going by pedaling with the foot on the side away from him while lifting the attacked foot and leg. We would shout at him, and somehow never got bit.

Mr. Hudson's father and mother, Mr. and Mrs. Press Hudson, lived in a big two-story house very near the road, and cousin Elise and Otha lived in a smaller log and frame house down a long driveway behind it. They were always there when we came. Often cousin Otha and Billy would be working on the school bus, and their other children would be helping around the house. They would take time off when we came. Cousin Elise did not want us to go to Pigg River, but she did not object to our going to the nearby Tomahawk Creek that flowed into the river a short distance from where we got to the creek. We, except the youngest, Carol, would walk up their driveway, across the road and down the hill to the creek and wade in it to the river. Pigg River was always reddish brown, and from Tomahawk Creek downstream to the "*Lews Island*" (Louis Island) covered bridge it was a good wading depth for us. There were a few deeper places that we avoided or floated through.

At the bridge the river banks were steep, but not too high for us to climb and then swing on a rope tied to near the top of an overhanging tree. A perfect place to grab the rope, walk with it up the sloping hill a little way, run down toward the river and swing out high over the water before letting go. We took turns "cannon balling" into the river while laughing and shouting. We also explored the old covered bridge. It had big beams supporting the floor and roof, and it had board-covered sides on the upper half and a railings along the lower sides. We would each throw a stick from the railing to race them to a picked place downstream. The bridge was too high and the water too shallow for us to jump from the bridge.

The way back up the river and creek was a harder journey. We always had gone to the "creek" and had a good time.

I was diagnosed with appendicitis during the latter part of the summer and had surgery by Dr. Bowen in the Danville Memorial Hospital. Another sickening experience with the ether anesthesia. This time there were several stitches to close the incision and a longer hospital stay of about a week to recover well enough to remove the stitches. During my hospital recovery, I read my first book, "Wings", and I was captive to a visiting preacher. The preacher took advantage of me as his helpless prey to forcefully declare his view of religion. I was glad when he left.

Not long before school started in 1938, Mother said that Daddy wanted her to go to Baltimore and live. She said that she did not want to go unless at least one of us children would go with her. Katie liked Averett where she would be a Senior in the two-year junior college and wanted to finish there before going to another college for her bachelor's degree. Paul said that he had rather go back to Hargrave where he would be a senior. I had rather stay at Climax where I would be a sophomore, but I did not want Mother and Daddy to blame me for keeping Mother from living in Baltimore with Daddy. I said I would go.

Daddy was living on the fourth floor of the Hopkins Apartment Building on 31st Street between St. Paul and Charles Streets. It was two blocks from our previous apartment in Bradford Apartments and on the corner where the street car coming up St. Paul turned east along 31st Street. There were double deck buses on Charles Street. With just the three of us, we kept the one-bedroom apartment that Daddy had. Mother and Daddy had the bedroom: I slept on the sofa in the living/dining room: There was a kitchenette, and we shared the one bathroom. Daddy rode the streetcar and bus with me to high school, Baltimore City College, the first day and went in with me to be registered and assigned courses and a class schedule. He also had a note from Dr. Bowen stating that I should not have strenuous exercises such as gym and calisthenics.

The curriculum at Baltimore City College was mostly literature, arts and letters that prepared students for academic, business, law and medicine. The curriculum at the other high school for white students, Polytechnic, prepared students for careers in engineering and mechanics. I don't know where the colored students went. Daddy took me to City College on Loch Raven Boulevard.

City College was a giant stone and red-brick four-story building with a tall bell tower. It sat on a hill up from the street with a long walk having two or three levels reached with steps to the main entrance. The enrollment was 2,500 boys -- no girls. There was an all-girl high school, Eastern, across Loch Raven. No trespassing between schools! From day one, I was lost. From about 100 high school students at Climax, all of whom I knew, to 2,500 boys who were all strangers and changing classes on four different floors had me in a confused state. I knew how to get to school and back and did a better job of understanding their "language." Maybe if I worked hard at studying I could get by. I had made my choice, and I was self-compelled to do the best I could to "finish what I had started." A trait that was already ingrained in my character by Mother.

Each week-day I would catch the street car after it made the turn from St. Paul onto 31st Street and ride to the bus stop on Greenmont Ave. where I transferred to the bus that took me to school. This route was reversed after school. There was a bakery and a grocery store where I got off the street car on 31st St. If I had money, sometimes I could not resist the bakery aroma and buy a cinnamon-raisin bun to take home with me. When I got to the apartment, I would listen to the radio while Mother prepared supper. Jack Armstrong, the All American Boy, sponsored by Wheaties, Little Orphan Annie and The Lone Ranger were the programs that were available on alternate afternoons at that time in the afternoon. I read the Baltimore Sun newspaper that came daily, and was very interested in the articles about a horse race at the Baltimore Pimlico race track. It was to be held November 1st. between Seabiscuit and triple crown winner War Admiral. There was a lot of information about both horses and the challenge between just the two in a "grudge" match. I listened to the race on the radio and was glad the underdog, Seabiscuit won. Each day when Daddy came from work, we ate supper and talked a little while before I did homework before going to bed on the sofa. Neither Mother or Daddy ever helped or showed interest in what my homework was; just that I did it.

I often quietly masturbated, but was surprised one night when I actually shot off a sticky, whitish liquid onto the sheet. A mess I had to clean up, and a new problem I had to solve. I quietly went to the bathroom and got toilet paper, and after wiping the sheet as dry as I could I flushed the paper down the toilet. Each night after that I took some toilet paper to bed with me. After my first panicky feeling, I felt a little proud to be gown up.

I found my class rooms and made it to each one before the bell. I got books and supplies. In addition to academic subjects, I also had one class a week of art. I did not take gym the first semester because of my appendicitis surgery. Instead, I had study hall. The only teacher's name I remember was my plane geometry teacher, Mr. Stoneseifer. My memory was reinforced by an embarrassing incident in his class when he called on me to go to the black board and prove one of the three theorems he had written there. I pointed and responded, "The one over yonder?" The whole class laughed hilariously. I was dumbfounded and asked, "Did I get the wrong one?" Mr. Stoneseifer did a poor job of trying not to laugh, and said, "No, you have the right one. It is just your accent." I went to the front of the class and proved the theorem correctly, but I may have been blushing the whole time.

I took my lunch, and ate in my home room which was also my English classroom. On nice days we could go outside for a short time after lunch, and I talked to some of the boys, but none of them lived near the Hopkins Apartment. The history lessons were mainly about Maryland. My art class was once each week, and I had difficulty remembering how to get there. I really liked the class and what the teacher was trying to teach. He gave us instructions in drawing and painting, and he was a skilled sculptor. He had done the large stone sculpture that was at the entrance of Eastern. The teacher could not control the other boys who would horse around and try to make a joke of his class.

Daddy rented a one-room apartment across the hall when Katie and Paul came for Christmas vacation. Paul and I slept in that apartment, and Katie took the sofa. Katie was surprised when she saw me and said, "You look like a peanut sitting on a watermelon." I had a small head size and had not noticed that I was that fat, even though I had gotten new clothes, and there were wear holes in my trouser legs just below my crotch where they had rubbed together. Mother was happy to have me eat the food she prepared, and the cinnamon-raisin buns helped too.

Daddy took us downtown to see the Christmas displays in department store windows and to do some Christmas shopping. Daddy said that he would wait for us at the entrance door of the Hub while we shopped. When I had purchased presents for Katie, Paul, Mother and Daddy, I went to the entrance door, and Daddy wasn't there. Katie and Paul were not there either. I looked outside up and down the street, and still couldn't see them. I finally realized that the merchandise and the store displays were not the same ones at the door we had gone in. I walked outside along the street by the Hub in the direction I thought I could find another door. The store continued around the street corner where I found a door where all of them were waiting for me. Daddy said that the Hub occupied a whole city block and had several entry doors. I wished he had told me that before I got lost.

We also watched the Christmas parade going down Charles Street. There were marching bands, decorated floats with people in costumes, tethered balloons of cartoon characters and a float with Santa and Mrs.

Claus. Daddy took pictures with his movie camera and included us in some of the scenes. Another treat was going downtown to a movie in a big movie theater, I think named Majestic. It was a huge auditorium with seats in the balcony around both sides and the back. Before the movie and between the main feature and short subjects, a man played a pipe organ on stage while the audience sang the words to the lyrics displayed on the screen. The display included a bouncing ball that bounced from one word to the next in the rhythm of the song. We went to an ice skating rink on North Ave. where we rented skates and tried to learn to not fall. I was sorry when Katie and Paul left and I had to go back to school.

When I returned to school I was required to take gym which also included swimming. This was another once-a-week class, but this was in the walk-out basement so I had no trouble remembering how to get to it. I don't remember which came first or if they were alternated by the week. Gym was a lot of running, calisthenics, parallel bars and rope climbing. I was not good at any of them and a complete failure trying to climb the rope. It was about 2 inches in diameter and hung from the ceiling to the floor. The exercise and test was to use only your hands and arms to climb as high as you could. I think all of the boys could go part way up and one or two made it to the ceiling. No matter how hard I tried, I could not get off the floor.

Swimming was better for me. The indoor, heated pool was large and had a locker room to put your clothes and a shower room with a line of showers. After undressing and going under a shower, we gathered in the water at the shallow end of the pool where the teacher gave us directions. We started with standing in the shallow water, submersing our heads and blowing bubbles. Then gradually during the next few months we did floating and swimming and progressing on to the Australian Crawl which required turning your head to one side to breath in and then turning it into the water to exhale in rhythm with your arm movements and kicking legs. I had never been swimming where all the boys were naked before, and it took a few classes for me to get comfortable doing so.

I gradually adjusted to school, and during the spring made friends with a boy who lived between the school and our apartment. Some days we would walk home together until we got to his house, and a few times I went inside with him. One time he came all the way to our apartment and came in. Otherwise, school was hard, but I did not have many distractions and made passing grades. Some days after school I would go across Charles Street to Wyman Park to walk around and watch people and birds. The Baltimore Museum at the north end of the park had a marble stature of Rodin's, *The Thinker,* at the foot of the stone stairs leading up to the entrance. Inside, there were some permanent paintings and artifacts and periodically some special temporary exhibits would be displayed. Usually on Sunday afternoons a WPA music group would present a concert. A Baptist church was across Charles Street from the museum. I went to a service there with Daddy once.

In the spring of 1939 the Sun published several articles about Adolph Hitler and the German army preparation for annexations of Czechoslovakia and Poland. They also published some articles about a new car that used very little amounts of gas and had the motor in the rear. They called it "Volkswagen." They also were working on a version that burned wood to heat water and run on steam. Other reported secret operations were some work on rockets, jet-powered airplanes and atomic bombs made from heavy water. These were very interesting to me, but England, France, Belgium and the rest of the European countries were extremely concerned. When Germany invaded and annexed part of Czechoslovakia in March of 1939, the English Prime Minister, Nevil Chamberlin, went to Germany and negotiated a treaty with Hitler that promised no interference from Europe and an agreement that Germany would cease any further attempts to annex any more territory. The newspaper photograph of Chamberlin carrying an umbrella became the symbol of a deriding "Appeasement" accusation. I was very much impressed by these news articles.

On nice Sunday afternoons, Daddy would get our car from the rented garage across 31st Street and take Mother and me for a ride. Daddy got a lot of pleasure testing my spelling ability by asking me to spell a word he had seen far ahead on a sign. Spelling was memorization, and that was something I did not do well. I spelled more phonetically than correctly and seldom got the right spelling. Daddy would laugh at my attempts. *Restaurant* was one misspelling that he laughed a lot about. I was glad that he did not get upset like he would have with Paul. We went to the Baltimore Zoo next to a reservoir some Sundays. The large animals were in outdoor pens, and the smaller ones and a few birds and fish were inside a big building. Visitors were allowed to feed peanuts to some of the monkeys.

One of Daddy's work associates who lived in a suburb of Baltimore had a daughter about my age and suggested that perhaps I might want to go with her and her younger sister ice skating on Saturday.

We met at the rink on North Avenue, and we had a good time. She already was a good skater and helped me learn some of the basics of staying upright and how to make skate strokes to move me along. Later near the end of school she invited me to attend a party at her school. It was at night, and Mr. Rogers and his daughter picked me up and brought me home. The party was in a decorated gymnasium and had music and some dancing. I really felt out of place, but she tried to teach me the basic "square" step and variations. She and her girlfriends were very friendly, and one asked, "Where did you find him?" I don't remember her answer. but it made me feel good.

I got my report card with all passing grades of my usual C's and D's. I think Mother and Daddy did not expect better, and I was glad that I passed.

Paul had graduated from Hargrave and was accepted at The University of Virginia, and Katie had finished two years at Averett Junior College and was accepted at Farmville State Teachers College. We spent the summer at Windcrest. Katie had a few dates with Dan Mattox, Arch Yeatts, Jr. and Harold Anderson. She had also had some dates with a boy in Danville. Paul had his driving license and dated Willie Francis Davis a few times. I was 15 and old enough to get my driving license.

I had been practicing driving and felt that I was ready for my test. Lieutenant George Moore, the State Policeman who gave the tests in Chatham, lived not far from us at Rondo. He had two daughters, Shine and Kitty. Kitty was Katie's age and had also dated Arch Yeatts, Jr. I parked in front of the court house and went into the jail office to submit my application. Lieutenant Moore accepted it and asked me a few questions about traffic signs and asked me to demonstrate hand signals for stopping and turning. I answered and demonstrated correctly. He got into the front passenger seat of our car and asked me to parallel park in front of the court house. I did that well enough. He then told me to drive north on Main Street. He watched the speedometer and my driving skills and told me to go all the way around the circle at the intersection of Main street with Military Drive and Holt Streets and then return to the court house. I passed the test and he gave me a temporary driver's license to use until my permanent one would arrive from Richmond. I did not get to drive much, but I had my license.

Sallie seemed to enjoy teaching first grade at Renan and living with the Parkers. She visited us once each summer when Lou came to visit, and she would bring little Paul with her for a few days. In June after she had been teaching two years, Mrs. Parker came to our house in a very agitated state looking for Sallie and her grandson, Junior. She said that both with baby Paul had left her house during the night a couple of days previously with Sallie taking some of her clothes and Junior only a tooth brush. She thought that they had eloped to get married, and she thought they might have come to our house. She blamed mother for having a daughter who would rob the cradle and marry someone ten years younger than she was. That was the first Mother had heard of Sallie's and Junior's romance and had no answers for Mrs. Parker. Mother was as flabbergasted as Mrs. Parker was irate. I stood silent wondering what would happen next. Nothing much. I think Mrs. Parker had run out of energy and just cried, and Mother seemed to sympathize with her while pleading innocence. Finally, Mrs. Parker left.

Later that summer, Sallie,Junior and little Paul came to our house and told Mother that they were in love and were married August 5, 1939. Junior was 18 and finished high school and was legal age as an adult to get married. Junior had been working for his grandfather who was was the supervisor of the State Department of Transportation for the Renan district and offered Junior a job doing road maintenance for the summer. Junior and Sallie both knew that Mr. and Mrs. Parker would never give their approval so they just eloped. Junior, who was Katie's age, seemed subdued and mostly listened while Sallie talked. They were living in a rental house near the Parkers.

Junior had some welding instructions and practice during his Agriculture shop classes and planned to work at the Newport News Ship Yard. The war in Europe had affected the military manufacturing industry in America, and Newport News Ship Yard was hiring workers.

Junior was hired to start in a welding training class in preparation for a regular job, and he Sallie and little Paul moved into a rental house in Newport News.

In addition to my house and farm chores that summer, Paul and I were given the job of painting the stable, corn and shop building, machinery/garage/grain house and the tenant house. The paint color for the first three was barn red and battle-ship gray for the tenant house. Daddy gave us a few instructions on painting and care of the paint and brushes at the end of a paint session. We were each to be paid 25 cents for an eight-hour day. That was the only paying job we had ever had, so we started with enthusiasm. I don't think either of us ever put in an 8-hour day. It was usually between 2 and 4 hours when it was not too hot.

Mother kept a record of our time, and marked it at 8-hour intervals. I painted from the ground up to step ladder height, and Paul painted the higher parts from an extension ladder. When he was high into the gables, I would hold the ladder to stabilize it. We worked on painting all summer and got it all done except the tenant house before school started. On Saturday afternoons mother would take us to Chatham where I would usually buy a banana split with one of my quarters at the soda fountain in Whitehead's Pharmacy.

Chapter 9

Hargrave and VPI

Commercial job

When school time approached in 1939, I said that I did not want to go back to Baltimore. Katie and Paul were going to college, so they did not have to choose. I enrolled at Hargrave as a Junior and had a room on Floyd Hall. Edward Otey Anderson, my second cousin and my age, was my roommate. His father, my Great Uncle Brigadier General (Retired) Edward Anderson, had died in 1937, and his mother, Aunt Amelia, had enrolled him. Edward's Grandmother, Mrs. Duncan, lived on Chalk Level Road just a short distance from Hargrave, and his Uncle, Charles Anderson, lived at Tomahawk.

Edward and I were the same age and got along well with each other. We gradually adjusted to the routine of military discipline and scheduling. I did not share many academic classes with him. I had Algebra under Major Tune, Bible under Captain Julius Spears, English under my cousin, Captain Cary Whitehead, who also was Military Commander, Biology under Captain Cheff and Latin under Major Brooks. Unexpectedly, I took an earnest interest in learning and gave more effort to studying. Getting A's and B's instead of my usual C's and D's put me on the honor roll for the first time in my educational experience. I never thought I could do it, and the good feeling gave me incentive to work harder. Latin was a tough subject that required an extra effort from me. It required a lot of memorization which I found I do not do easily. The old rhyme, "Latin is a dead language, dead as it can be; First it killed the Romans, now it's killing me." became a living truth for me. Learning English required some memorizing, but it was based on my earlier classes. Where I did best and actually enjoyed were Algebra and Biology. These two subjects were based on something physical and rational problem solving. There were few classroom distractions, class sizes were not over 20 students and the teachers gave an interest in helping students to learn.

My first cousin, Captain Cary Whitehead, was the Commandant and military teacher. He had graduated from The Army Military Academy at West Point, New York, but decided he wanted to become a medical doctor instead of having a military career. While getting disengaged from the Army and getting enrolled in the University of Virginia medical school, he worked at Hargrave as Commandant and English teacher while the regular English teacher, his brother-in-law, was getting a masters' degree. Because he did not stay in the Army after receiving free education, I think Uncle Hurt had to reimburse the government for his education.

Another Chatham native, Captain Carlton White, had graduated from the University of North Carolina and was waiting to be accepted at the University of Virginia law school. Captain White was the track and field coach under head coach Captain Taylor Sanford. I was not a good athlete, but by helping with the track equipment I could work off demerits instead of the lengthier "Bull Ring" marching. After a set number of hours helping put up and put away hurdles. pole vault and high jumping equipment and marking lines for the running events, I would get credit for so many demerits. I liked Coach White and working with the track team and became manager. One of the things I did not like was the abusive way he treated Robert "Goat" Nash. Goat, who lived in Chatham and was the son of a rural mail carrier, had an athletic scholarship as aday student. He was a good athlete in several sports, but when Coach White thought he was not performing up to his potential, he verbally and physically attacked him. One time he was slapping Goat, and then he kicked him. I was helpless to do anything to appease my emotions except an ineffective effort to forget what I had seen. We stopped keeping a record of my time, and when I got demerits, he would give me a note of credit.

Edward had a strong interest in the outdoor natural environment, and the extra credits Captain Cheff gave for finding certain specimens of wild flora and fauna stimulated both of us to spend free time exploring the farms and streams behind the campus. One of our enjoyable places was Moses Mill on Cherrystone Creek and just across the Southern Railway tracks from school. The mill was usually closed when we went there so it was a quiet place except for the water pouring over the dam. There were some times when water moccasin snakes would be sunning on the abutments of the dam. We did not disturb them and waded in the shallow flowing water downstream from the dam. Fish trying to get upstream were blocked by the dam and would be trapped in the deeper pools of Cherrystone Creek. On one visit after missing a couple, we caught a couple of 16-inch catfish. We put them on a forked small branch and took them back to school and persuaded the dietitian to cook them for our supper. Other times we would find crayfish, salamanders, snails, bird's eggs, wild flowers, etc. for extra credit. Another cadet, Bill Hathaway, went with us a few times.

Crossing the rail road tracks was interesting as a side attraction.

Trying to see how far we could walk a rail before falling off and putting pennies on a track before a steam engine came roaring by to leave a flattened and elongated penny. We would also put our ear on the steel rail and listen for the vibrations of an approaching train long before we could hear it. Then we noticed the change in pitch of the sound from high to low as it went past us.

Edward got permission to visit his Grandmother Duncan on a few weekends, and sometimes he would walk there for the day. I went with him once for an overnight stay. Mrs. Duncan had a house servant, and we were well fed. Mrs. Duncan lived in a white, big two-story house with a two story front porch and supporting columns. Her farm included the remnants of a water-powered grist mill beside a creek and a broken rock dam. During my visit, Edward and I explored the farm and mill site and talked about his mother, her sister and his deceased grandfather. We did not talk about his deceased father.

On one special weekend at Hargrave, Edward's mother and sister, Fanny, came. They were allowed to visit in the dormitory rooms to see how we lived. Fanny was a couple of years older than Edward and me, and she was really, really beautiful. A blond with blue eyes and dimples when she smiled. Their tour and visit only lasted one day, but Edward got requests from several cadets for an introduction to Fanny.

I made good grades and finished my junior year at Hargrave and wanted to go to summer school to take solid geometry and trigonometry. That way I would not need to have extra subjects to graduate the next regular school year. I had my driver's license so I drove our car to school and back. Girls were allowed as day students during the summer session, and Lucy Charles Jones attended along with me and some other local boys and boarding foreign boys. One of the boys was Marse Ferrell who I had known in fifth grade in Chatham. The class times were longer than during the regular school year, and the two-subject curriculum was over at lunch time. Most times we staid a little while to talk before starting home.

I wanted to learn how to play the piano, and I found a piano teacher in Chatham that scheduled lessons in her home twice each week for me. I took my lunch on those days, and had my lesson after I had eaten. I learned the rudiments of the piano as a musical instrument and written music. Putting music from the written page into audible music was a structured process for me. I could read the notes and press the correct keys to match, but timing and rhythm did not follow. I found that becoming a piano player would take more time and effort than I wanted to give, so I discontinued the lessons in favor of my two academic subjects.

Marse's mother, Marguerite, had gotten her divorce and married my first cousin, Claude Whitehead. For a couple of years, they had been living in San Salvador where Claude had been a tobacco buyer for American Tobacco Company. Claude had retired, and they were living in Chatham while waiting for their house to be built on their farm. Some days after school I would give Marse a ride home and go in for a while. They lived in the apartment over cousin "Duke" and Anna Kenny on Lanier Ave. Claude showed me the blue prints for the house they were building and pointed out some of its features.

One Saturday, Marse came to Windcrest for a day's visit. Katie,

Paul, Marse and I played croquet and ping pong. Paul and Marse were both good players and had close matches. I was not as good, and I did not have as an aggressive desire to win. Paul, Marse and I did some target shooting with Paul's 22 rifle. We all were good at hitting a stationary target, so we started shooting at a tin can thrown into the air. One of us would throw the can up for another to shoot at. We did better as we got experience. Mother served a good dinner, and Marse left a couple of hours later. Summer school continued, and having Lucy Charles to talk and joke with helped make the recess between classes enjoyable.

Late in the summer I went for an overnight at Marse's new home. It was right out of the old southern mansions. It was off route 57 east into a long driveway lined with water oaks on each side up a slight grade to a circle driveway in front of a tall-columned front porch in to a very large brick house. The central hall had rooms on both sides and in the back. The gently rising and curved stairway with banisters on one side went up to the open balcony that had doors to bedrooms and bath rooms. The tall entry hall had an ornate chandelier hanging from a long chain. The kitchen and breakfast room were at the back of the entry hall. Claude and Marguerite showed me that they were glad I had come and showed me to my room and gave a tour of the rest of the house. They had a house servant/cook who served supper in the breakfast room. There was no formality. Claude talked about farming and his Milking Shorthorn dairy he was just getting started. Marse and I walked around outside in the yard which rose from the road in front and from Banister River in back. There were big open farm fields in three directions and trees to the east.

After breakfast the next morning, Marse and I went to his

grandmother Motley's house not far away on Motley's Mill Road. Marse had a rifle that we took to hunt squirrels in the woods on the farm. We saw one, and Marse missed it. We continued walking and looking and came to a tenant house where an older black lady was in her yard. She knew Marse and offered us a drink of blackberry wine she had made. We each took a sip as she continued telling us about Marse's uncles Blair and Latne Motley who used to come by her house and drink her wine.

When we got back to Mrs. Motley's it was dinner time. We washed our hands and sat at her dining room table where her house maid/cook served us old-fashioned southern food. A couple of dogs waited near the table until someone dropped some food on the floor. This was real old fashioned southern aristocratic living which I thought had passed. After dinner, Marse and I went out under some big shade trees where the farm workers were taking a long rest during the heat of the day. They were pitching horse shoes. They would encourage the horse shoes to be a ringer by talking and laughing as they pitched. They let Marse and me pitch a game or two with them before we left to go back to Marse's house.

I had good grades in summer school and started my senior year in 1940 with Edward as my roommate on Floyd Hall again. A few days after school started, I was given a promotion to 2nd. lieutenant in charge of the junior school cadet Company C. I had to live in the Junior School dormitory and would share a room with a high-school junior, Guy Ed Hairston, as my staff sergeant. When I moved, Bill Hathaway moved in with Edward. Bill was from Danville and an aspiring naturalist. He and Edward were very compatible in that way.

My classes were English under my cousin Captain Kenny who had taken the previous year to go to graduate school, Physics and Chemistry under Captain Cheff, Latin 2 under Major Brooks and American History under Colonel Floyd. I also had responsibility for teaching and training military maneuvers, neatness, schedule structure and discipline to about 30 junior school cadets. The day started at reveille and a march in formation to breakfast, and it ended with taps and lights out. Guy helped me, and we two became good friends.

At parades as an officer, I got to wear knee-high black boots with riding britches and a saber with scabbard and supporting Sam Brown shoulder belt. As a senior, I also got to replace my overcoat with a cape. I was a little disappointed when I was only promoted to a 1st. lieutenant instead of a captain as some previous Company C officers had been. I did not complain and hoped I would perform well enough to get another promotion.

Marse was a day student so I usually only saw him in classes that we both had, and my being in the junior building and with junior-school cadets separated me from cadets in the high school barracks. My contact with Edward and his roommate, Bill Hathaway, was limited to a few times when we would be on the front lawn or at the swimming pool. Bill had caught a puff adder snake about two feet long and kept it in a cage in his and Edward's room. When we were hidden behind trees and he released it near the middle of the lawn, it would look around for a hiding place and start crawling for cover. Then when we appeared, it would gasp and curl in an anguished display and fall back and appear dead. It could have gotten an acting award if one was available for snakes. Bill and

Edward continued walking "nature trails", but I did not have time to go with them.

I really liked my physics class and teacher, Captain Cheff. Most of the physics was about physical things that I could relate to. Optical and mechanical lessons were about things I could see and visualize the explanations of the way they worked. Lessons about electrical properties and interaction were somewhat less physical in that only the effects could be seen and measured. The laboratory part of the class stimulated my desire to learn more of the "what and how" things happened. I had similar interests in my chemistry class. Latin was a very different subject, and I had to study hard to stay on the honor roll.

Captain Kenny taught both grammar and literature in my senior English class, and we were required to write essays. Both Marse and Edward were in that class with me, but there was not much time for us to associate together.

For Christmas vacation that year in 1940, Mother and Daddy picked up Paul, Katie and me from our schools, and we went to Miami Beach, Florida. We stopped overnight in Brunswick, Georgia, and the next day we got to Miami Beach. We did not have reservations, so Daddy would leave us in the car while he went in to check availability, prices and general appearance. After finding "mostly northern Jews" in the beach-front hotels, he found what suited him at a hotel, Peter Miller, that was not on the beach but had an arrangement for their guests to use the beach of one of the beach-front hotels. Daddy rented an apartment, and we unpacked and cleaned up a little and then drove up Collins Avenue looking for a restaurant. Daddy selected Jack Dempsey, and we found good food at a reasonable price. Mother got food from a grocery store for most of our meals.

After a night's sleep and breakfast, we were ready for the ocean and beach. Mother was not feeling well and stayed in the apartment. It was amazing to be on a warm, sandy, salt-water ocean beach at Christmas time. Daddy and we three siblings waded in the warm shallow water and rode gentle waves. We washed the salt water off under cold, fresh water at a beach-side shower, and then lay on towels for a sun tan/burn. A lazy happy day to build an appetite. We did not have a "night life": just talking until bed time. Katie was a senior at Farmville and had been engaged to a divinity student she met while going to Averett College. When she found he had been dating another girl while she was in college at Farmville, she broke the engagement. Paul talked some about being a student at the University of Virginia and about his roommate. I did not have much to say about Hargrave because they already knew about Hargrave.

On the day after Christmas we three siblings went on a boat ride on Indian Creek that ran length wise up the middle of the Miami Beach island. The elaborate Christmas house and boat dock decorations seemed out of place in such a bright sunshine and warm place with palm trees, blooming flowers and green grass. Mother was still sick, so it was just Daddy and us three siblings at the beach and on a drive around Miami. There were brightly painted houses and lots of tropical flowers and shrubs along with palm trees. The long driveway to Hialeah race track was lined with white-trunk Royal Palm trees.

We left Miami Beach on the 31st of December and stopped to tour Saint Augustine. We saw the Castillo de San Marcos fort, Ripley's

Believe It or Not museum and took a drink from Ponce de Leon's Fountain of Youth. Katie, Paul and I went on a horse-drawn carriage ride before we left for Brunswick, Georgia for the night. Daddy took a lot of pictures with his movie camera during our Christmas vacation in Florida. Not much sleep in Brunswick because of New Year celebrations, but with Paul driving some we got to Windcrest before dark.

My class work went well, and, except for one incident, my supervision of the military responsibility of the junior cadets did also. One 7th-grade cadet, Goetz, became upset about a perceived unfair demerit I had given him. On a Saturday morning he came into our room and started an argument by telling me how incompetent I was and that all the cows backed up to a stump when I went home to my farm. I had heard that statement before as a joke, but When he called me a "fairy", I did not know what that meant. Then he started shoving and hitting me. We had a small room so the "fight" did not have much room to maneuver or strike hard blows. Guy separated us, and got him to leave. I had a sore place or two but no bruises other than to my emotions. When I asked Guy if I had done alright in the tussle, he said that I had. I also asked if a fairy was the same as a sissy? Guy said that a fairy was someone who liked other boys. I was shy around girls, but a long, long way from being a fairy.

Mother's oldest sister, Aunt Nannie, had retired from her government job in Washington and was living in her house on Main Street. She invited me to visit her one Sunday afternoon. I did not know her very well, but she was friendly and seemed very glad to see and talk with me. She served cookies and lemon aide and told me some things about her family when she was growing up. She had taught school when

Mother was a student of hers. She also told me about her father, my Grandfather. She had the saber he had during the Civil War and the bullet removed from him after he was shot. She did not say in which battle he was wounded, but did continue to tell me that the bullet had entered his abdomen from the front and had lodged just under his skin in his back. I coveted those heirlooms.

I wanted to make some money to have when I started college in the fall. The father of a junior-school cadet, Bo Sapp, was a Naval officer who was supervising the work of a contractor that was building a new dry dock in the Norfolk Navy Yard in Portsmouth, Virginia. I talked with Bo about whether the contractor his father oversaw might be willing to give me a job for the summer. When his father came on a visit, I talked with him, and he said that he was sure I would have a job. He gave a date and address for me to report to. I had been accepted by the Virginia Military Institute (VMI) and was looking forward to majoring in some type of engineering.

Graduation time was coming, and warm spring weather brought out the "silly" in me. One evening after taps and every one was asleep, Guy and I stripped naked and ran across the front lawn to the swimming pool. After swimming across the pool a few times, we ran back to the Junior-school building and quietly sneaked to our room. It was exciting not to be caught breaking the rules with punishable consequences.

Senior class honor offices were determined by grade averages. Marse had the highest and earned Valedictorian which required him to give a speech during the graduation ceremony. Marse was very smart, and he was very, very shy in public. He refused to give the Valedictory speech. The class president gave a speech instead. I received my diploma, and Katie received a Bachelor of Arts degree in education from Farmville State Teacher's college. Paul had finished his sophomore year at the University of Virginia.

I was at home for a few days before taking the bus to Lou's in Norfolk. We found a newspaper ad for room and board in Portsmouth. I called and made an appointment to see it. It was on a bus line to the place I would be working, had a vacant small room and furnished breakfast, dinner and a packed lunch. There were other men boarders in other rooms so we shared the bathroom. The price was acceptable so I paid the advance rent and unpacked my bag.

I reported to work and was told that because I was a temporary employee, I would not have to join the union. Also, I was given a salary of $125/month as a carpenter's helper instead of an hourly wage. I was assigned to a work crew supervised by Mr. Johnson, a man with a Swedish accent from Minnesota. He was gruff and demanding, but he knew how to build the work barges needed for use in building the cofferdam (temporary dam) for a new Navy dry dock. My job was to keep the carpenters supplied with lumber, nails and other materials and to clean the work area. Their work station was near the end of a temporary pier where the finished barges could be launched into the water. It was heavy work carrying some of the lumber, and it was hot in the sunshine. My baseball cap did not shield my nose and ears, and they blistered and pealed for the first week until the skin toughened and browned. I kept busy all day, and was glad to get "home" in the evening. We usually worked on Saturday and only had Sundays off. The carpenters and I were glad for the over-time pay. I was friendly with other workers, but I did not have any local friends. A few Sundays I visited Lou in Norfolk, and once I received a phone call from Robert telling me that Lou and he had been in a car wreck. Lou's head had gone through the windshield, and in addition to bruises to her head, broken glass had cut her face and around her neck. I went to the hospital and found that the cuts were very close to a main artery in her neck, but did not cut it. Robert had sisters that took care of Bobby Lou and Lou while she healed.

About half way through the summer, one of the two boarders in the room across the hall from me left. My landlady asked if I would share the room at a lower rent so she could find another boarder for my room. The remaining boarder, "Slim", and I had become friends so it was an easy decision for us. Slim Baker was about 10 years older than me, and he was about 30 years ahead of me in life experiences. He was an electrician working in the Navy Yard, but not at the location where I was. He had been a merchant marine, and his previous job had been as an electrician at Cape Canaveral, Florida where a new, large air base was being constructed. We became good friends and got to know a lot about each other. One Sunday Slim took another boarder and me in his Ford Model A car to a pier near the mouth of the James River. We rented a small outboard motor boat and fishing equipment, and we bought some bait. We actually caught a few keeper-size fish which we took to our landlady. That was our only outing.

I had been accepted by VMI and had planned to start there, but I found that their engineering program did not offer a degree in Electrical Engineering. I had also applied to and had been accepted by Virginia

Polytechnic Institute (VPI) which did offer a degree in Electrical Engineering. I notified VPI that I would enroll there in September.

I made a bus trip home during the July 4th holiday, but otherwise for the entire summer it was all work with only a brief couple of days off. While I was at home I found out that Jewel had won the Miss Pittsylvania County contest and would compete for the state Miss Virginia title.

I quit my job a couple of weeks before I was scheduled to start at VPI and spent that time at home. Katie got a job teaching fourth grade at Whitmell Farm Life High School in Pittsylvania County. It was about five miles west of Danville. I helped her move her things to a boarding house near the school. During the summer, Daddy had given each of his five children $5,000. I used mine to start a savings account at Planters Bank in Chatham.

Marse had been accepted at VPI and planned to major in Chemical Engineering. His mother, Marguerite, was going to take him and asked me to go with them. It was a full day of travel and enrolling. Marse and I went through the lines to register and get room and military unit assignments. Both of us were assigned to the same building on the upper quadrangle, but to different Coast Guard Batteries. Marse was in I Battery on one end of the building, and I was in K Battery on the other end. We were also given a curriculum with class schedules. Each had to buy a new mattress which we put on the top of Marguerite's car to take to the entrance of the upper quadrangle. There we said goodbye, and I gave my thanks to Marguerite. We carried our things and found our rooms in time for supper.

I had a large corner room on the first floor that I shared with two other freshman cadets, Thompson and Starling. I had the single cot and they had the two-deck bunk bed. Our uniforms from the supply store were tried on for proper fit. The style was different from the Hargrave uniform, and the color was Union blue instead of Confederate gray. There was a "ranking" sophomore and some other sophomores that gave us military instructions and indoctrination. It was impressed on us that we were "rats" and lower than that most despised filthy creature. At all times on the quadrangle we marched in a "brace" with stiff straight back, head up straight and pulled back so that the chin was against the Adam's apple. Shoulders had to be straight and in a strain to have the shoulder blades touch each other. No casual walking or running from entering the quadrangle to entering the barracks. Our uniform had to be clean and pressed, and our shirt had to be tucked in and "pleated" tight around the waist. Shoes and leather belt had to be polished and our caps had to be worn at all times and in the prescribed way.

Strict military discipline required subservience to all upper classmen and a salute to all officers. Room cleanliness and order were available for inspection at all times and required coming to attention when an upperclassman entered. Periodic military discipline "instruction" sessions were given by assembling all rats in the Battery into a larger over-heated corner room. Rats were in full woolen uniform, including overcoats and brought to a bracing attention while sophomores energetically, in-your-face, shouted demeaning insults. Of course, the sophomores were dressed casually, but there were a couple of juniors encouraging (threatening) the sophomores to be more vigorous. I started feeling sort of being somewhere in a dream, similar to the way I felt when

I fainted on the parade field at Hargrave on a hot day after a big lunch. Another cadet was first to pass out and taken to the hall and revived. This ended the session.

General engineering courses were my curriculum for the first year. I had to struggle with my classes and was glad I had been at Hargrave my junior and senior years of high school. I went along OK with the military system and did not receive much extra attention.

The annual Thanksgiving football rivalry between VPI and VMI was played in the Roanoke Stadium. The cadet corps of both schools attended. VPI cadets rode the "Huckleberry" train from Blacksburg to the Roanoke train station and then marched in formation to the stadium. On the train and at the stadium, we chanted school slogans, "Hokie, Hokie, Hokie high, Hang them low, Hang them high, Hokie, Hokie, Hokie high" or something like it, and others. In the stadium, rats sat in the lower rows with upper classmen behind where they berated the rats to shout and cheer. It was a nice, sunshiny day, and at half time, the VPI "Highty-Tighty" marching band of about a hundred members paraded and played. They were followed by The VMI band of about 20 performing adult non-cadets. I do not remember much about the game or who won. I was glad when it ended. Daddy had come to attend the game and to take me home for the short Thanksgiving holiday. We found each other on the playing field among the celebrating and leaving cadets and parents.

Thanksgiving at home with Katie, Paul, Mother and Daddy, and the home-gown turkey for the holiday meal were all reasons to celebrate, enjoy and give thanks for. The time was short, and it went too fast. Marguerite took Marse and me to the bus station in Roanoke instead of

159

taking us all the way to Blacksburg. When we got to the bus station, Marguerite waited to go home until after we purchased our tickets. Marse and I each had a sandwich and a drink from the lunch counter before the bus was ready to leave. Marse was ahead of me in the line to get on the bus, and when I boarded, all the seats were taken except some space on the back bench. I took my suit case and went there and sat. After all the passengers were boarded, the bus driver turned to look toward the back of the bus and shouted, "You back there, come up here to the front." He waited and said, " You can't sit back there." I wasn't sure he was talking to me, so I said, "Who? me?" He said, "Yes, you cannot sit in the colored section." I said, "I don't mind sitting here." He said, "You will either come to the front, or I will have the police take you off this bus." That got my attention. It was dark, and I did not want to spend the night in jail, so I went and stood in the aisle just behind the driver.

Another cadet from Chatham was Henry Carter. He was a senior majoring in Agriculture and was in a barracks on the lower campus. Henry had ridden his horse the 100 miles from Chatham and had it stabled at the campus horse barn. He sometimes would ride around the campus and have the horse rear up and paw the air. Henry had done similar "shows" in downtown Chatham.

The end of the first quarter was getting close when on Sunday, December 7 there was a news report on the radio that Japan had bombed Pearl Harbor in Hawaii. Shortly after that announcement, President Franklin D. Roosevelt made a speech describing the surprise attack and declared that it was "A Day of Infamy" and an act of war. VPI was a Reserve Officer Training Corps (ROTC) school that granted academic degrees and also reserve commissions in the military. The seniors were expecting to be commissioned as officers and called into active duty immediately after graduation. I was 17 and all members of the corps of cadets were of military age. Excitement and uncertainty ruled the minds of cadets and faculty. Exams were just a week or two away, so last-minute studying gave some structure toward normalcy.

There was no reprieve from normal military discipline. Rats were still rats, and the harassment continued. After the last exam, rats were given a Christmas gift by upper classmen wielding belts and brooms. When I got to my barracks, a riot of upperclassmen was armed and dangerous. Some had belts, but most had brooms. Rats were ordered to grab their ankles. I was fresh flesh and was knocked forward almost off my feet by the first swing of the broom. They did not stop until all the sophomores on my floor had given me my " Christmas present." I "took it like a man" and got my suit case packed. My buttock was numb for a short time before I felt the pain. I rode the bus home for Christmas vacation and stood up a lot of the trip. The soreness gradually went away, and the black and blue slowly turned to yellow/tan before my behind was normal again.

Chapter 10

Civilian and Biology Student

Double change

Christmas was a good break from college. Paul had a couple of dates with Willie Frances, and Marse arranged a date for us with two girls in Danville. We went in Marse's car and spent a very casual evening with them at his girl's house. It was also a time to talk about the war. Each county was forming a "Draft Board" that required all males between the ages of 16 and 40 to register. Because both Paul and I were in college, we thought we would get a deferment. Paul was thinking about volunteering in the Army Air Force.

It was a cold winter in Blacksburg, and marching to the mess hall on the lower campus in snow was misery. Even my assigned table, place and table etiquette were " controlled" by an upper-class man. Freshmen were served last from the passed- around food dishes, and we had to sit at attention on the edge of our chairs while we ate. If we committed any infraction of the rules we were required to eat a "square" meal by moving our eating utensil up-and-in at right angles from plate to mouth.

All of my classes were around the drill field, and chemistry was at the far end near the "Duck Pond." Getting to the next class on time between classes required me to hurry. I was doing alright with my grades and liked the challenge of calculus. Instead of static number manipulation, lessons involved varying rates and changes. Most text books were written to be used in the college academic 2-semester system, but VPI used them on a 3-quarter system. Some classes pushed to cover the semester lessons into a quarter. Lewis Gregory who lived on a farm near Marse was in one of my classes. His two older brothers, Stone and

James, had been called into the army, and their father had applied to the draft board for a deferment for Lewis to help him on the farm. At the end of the second quarter Lewis left VPI and went home to farm.

Lou's husband, Robert, had a job in Norfolk as ticket agent for a railway company. He was transferred to Atlanta, but the job did not last long. He then worked as a manager of a Piggly Wiggly grocery store where he soon got one of the cashiers pregnant. Lou divorced him and was working in a furniture store when she met and Married Bob Culpepper. Bob had not been married before and was the manager of the hardware department of Sears & Roebuck. They wanted to buy Tuxedo Hardware in the Buckhead area of Atlanta. Daddy loaned them $10,000, and she asked me to loan her my $5,000. She would pay interest and pay me back in a couple of years. I agreed since I would not need the money while I was in school.

During my time at home at the end of my second quarter, I applied for and received an educational deferment if I remained in college. Also, I found out that Jewel and Mr. Gordon Trent had become lovers and that Jewel was pregnant. Mr. Trent's wife had been working in Dr. Hammer's office in Chatham and was so devastated by her husband's infidelity she committed suicide by taking some pills. Jewel and Mr. Trent married shortly after Mrs. Trent's death. I was emotionally distressed that Jewel was now married, but I had not made any effort to get in contact with her other than one letter I sent to her when I first got to VPI. I was struggling to get through college and had no time or money to have a meaningful relationship, and I did not want just a casual one. Losing a possibility with her really hurt.

163

Some of the upperclassmen were natural bullies and took the opportunity to show just how sadistic they could become with the encouragement of the system. After exams before the Christmas holiday, freshmen were literally paddled with brooms and broom handles until our behinds were bruised and some bleeding from beatings by multiple sophomores. That treatment and the constant harassment caused some students to seek a college education elsewhere, while some stayed until finishing their freshman year before transferring. The admonition from my mother, "When you start something, you must finish it" gave me determination, and I thought that other friends and relatives from my community had endured and I must be able to do so too. Having an older dominant brother also helped prepare me.

When I moved from the three-mate room with Thompson and Stalling, I moved to share a basement room with L. J. Hamlett who lived at Ripplemead, a short distance up a mountain road from Pearisburg and not far west from Blacksburg. I took the top bunk in this much smaller room. The basement was not completely below ground level, and our room had a window near the ceiling. LJ was the opposite of an outspoken extrovert and had the nick name, Mousy. We got along well as roommates and friends. LJ's father was manager of a lime kiln which was located not far from their house. When I visited LJ one weekend I could see the bare side of the mountain where the lime stone was blasted from and down to near the kiln. His father came to get us and brought us back at the end of the weekend. I had a good time, and his parents treated me very nicely. They had a 22-cal. pistol which LJ and I used to shoot at targets. His mother was severely incapacitated and in pain from arthritis and had trouble moving around. The New River gorge and mountains were beautiful and a contrast to Windcrest.

There was a sophomore who had selected me as his special target to nit pic and harass. There was nothing I could do to please him or to stop his aggressive behavior toward me. The only chance I had to get revenge was by not being caught while "water-bedding" him. With LJ as my accomplice, I had found a janitor's bucket in the bathroom and filled it with water before we went to bed. About an hour later at the time of deepest sleep, LJ and I were barefoot and went to the bathroom where I got the bucket. All the time checking that we were not seen or heard, he went first up the stairs to the second floor. No one was in the hall, so LJ silently proceeded to our target's door. I was ready with the water when LJ silently turned the knob and shoved the door open at which moment I threw the whole bucket of water on the sleeping target. LJ had started running after he shoved the door open. I was in hot pursuit to catch up. We were back in bed by the time we heard commotion on the upper floors and then in the basement floor. Two sophomores came into our room and "woke" us from a deep sleep and questioned us and then ordered us to get out of bed. They then felt the sheets in our beds and found they were too warm for us to be the culprits. They left, and my heart rate slowly returned to normal before I finally honestly fell asleep.

To accelerate the education process, VPI and other colleges eliminated summer vacations. There would be continuous quarters with three still required as a school year. At the end of my freshman year there were only a few days of vacation before the next quarter began.

Sophomores in each Company or Battery were ranked based on

their grade in the Military class and on academic grades. The highest ranking was the "ranking" sophomore. I had an A or two, but most of my grades were Bs and Cs, so I was surprised to be third ranking in K Battery. Marse would have been the ranking sophomore in I Battery if he had returned. Marse was very smart in more than academics: he had chosen to transfer to Carnage Institute in Pittsburgh.

Instead of the wool uniforms, we had cotton, light-weight ones for the summer quarter. My electrical engineering course required classes in general engineering subjects of surveying and engineering mechanics in addition to introduction to electrical circuits. We had classroom instruction and we used transits and tapelines to survey the drill field. My mechanics class was taught by professor Raush. Rumors were that he did not have a college degree but had performed so well for Packard Motor Company that he was on a retainer with them and was given a faculty job at VPI. He frequently expressed his hatred for sophomores. We were the scum of mankind, mostly because of the way we treated freshmen. He had a wooden pointer that he used to point to illustrations on the blackboard, and when he could see waning attention among the students, he would strike it vigorously across his or a front-row student's desk. All the students nearly fell off their high stools as they jumped in response to the noise. He knew his subject, and he demanded attention. He also made learning mechanics interesting. I also took engineering drawing. Using lettering guides with dip-pen India ink on vellum resulted in a lot of wasted vellum.

My third cousin, Edward Blair, was a freshman in K Battery. He was my age and had graduated from Climax and then went to Hargrave for a year of postgraduate education to better prepare him for college. His father, William (Cousin Bill), had married my second cousin, Isabelle Anderson, and Edward was the youngest of several children. Cousin Bill had been ranking cadet and corps Colonel when he graduated from VPI, and Edward had an older brother who had graduated from VPI and was a Colonel in the army. I limited my association with Edward as a "rat" to not bring attention to our friendship and consequently more harassment to him.

Along in the late fall of his first year and my second, K Battery had a "special instruction session" for rats. It was a repeat of what I had been through a year earlier except this time I was the aggressor and Edward and his classmates were the harassed. The hot and crowded corner room and wool uniforms with overcoats for the freshman were standard. A junior supervisor demanded sophomores be more aggressive until Edward fainted. I helped pull him into the hall and loosened his clothes to help revive him. I said, "I am very sorry." He responded, "That's OK." I really felt sorry for him and hated myself for treating him and others this way. It was easier for me to take the punishment than to meet it out. I received more demerits my first quarter as a sophomore than I had gotten for my entire 3 quarters as a freshman.

On Christmas vacation in 1942 I had my first official date. Jacqueline Hudson was a couple of years younger than me, and as children we had played together in family groups. I used our car to drive to her Grandmother's house where she was staying. Her Grandmother served some desert and a drink and then she went to bed. We sat on the sofa and talked about what we had been doing since we last had been together in school and play. She would graduate from Climax in the coming May and did not have plans beyond that. As I said goodnight we kissed, and I left.

Katie had unpleasant discipline problems teaching school. She was small, and some of her aggressive pupils were larger than she was. When her year of teaching was over, she started working at Dan River Mills in Danville and living in the company-owned apartment building, Hilton Hall, in Schoolfield. Caroline Yeatts was working and living there too. Caroline was single but had an affair with a young man and got pregnant. The man did not want to get married, and Caroline did not want to have the baby. Caroline's uncle, Dr. John Anderson, Jr., either performed the abortion or had a fellow surgeon abort the fetus in the Memorial Hospital. Katie had a date to attend a Christmas dance in the Danville Armory, and she made a date for me to take Caroline. I used our car to take the four of us to the decorated ballroom and live band music. My poor dancing skills did not do much for me during our time on the dance floor, and Caroline responded as a friend and neighbor. It was a nice outing for me, and, against advice from Katie and others, Caroline was still friendly with her ex-boyfriend.

In contrast to Caroline's pregnancy, another neighbor, Ruth Bailey, had gotten pregnant. Ruth was about my age and the daughter of Tom Bailey and had three older brothers with questionable character. She also had a physically deformed and mentally challenged sister. When a car would stop in their yard at night and blow the horn, Ruth would happily ride away with the man inside. I don't think anyone ever admitted to being her baby's father, but it was rumored to be her first cousin,

Junior Smith. Ruth did not have parents who cared much about her condition, and she did not have a caring physician uncle. She birthed her baby boy who developed with the stigma of "bastard" and was reared by his grandparents. Ruth later married a neighbor, Hilton Walker. When Ruth was pregnant while living with him, she was "accidentally" shot in the stomach with a 22-cal. rifle.

My class in electric circuits had gone well for the first and second quarters using vacuum tubes, resistors and voltage dividers. Getting into magnetism, phase changes and things that I had trouble visualizing was very difficult for me. LJ was majoring in Pre-Med in the Biology Department. It was a subject with a lot of Latin words, and largely was about something physical. Also, the military branches were in such need of medical professionals that they offered free school expenses to their members who were accepted to medical school. I inquired at the Biology Department about my transferring from Electrical Engineering and found that I would get credit for all the classes I had taken. I could take the Chemistry and Biology classes I had missed instead of elected classes and would have enough credits to graduate with my class. I changed my major at the end of my second year.

I was with a new group of classmates at the Biology and Chemistry buildings, and it was a long walk from the upper quadrangle. I found out that the military at VPI no longer offered ROTC officer commissions because the Army needed more officers faster than the ROTC could furnish. Instead, a 90-day training program had been established to train officers. Since I had satisfied my 2-year VPI-required military training, and staying in the military corps would not result in a

169

commission, I started looking for a rental room in town. I was glad when my second year was complete so I was not required to stay in the corps of cadets.

One of my new classmates had recently made the move I was planning and offered to share his room with me. Arthur Connor, *"AC"*, was from Chatham and had found a room in the basement of a house on east Main Street in return for firing a coal-burning furnace. The landlady, Mrs. Johnson, was the widow of a VPI professor. In return for my room, I agreed to help with the furnace.

I withdrew from the military and moved in with AC. It was a large basement room with private bath room. It had a private outside entry through the furnace room to a door at the back of the house. Although there was a stairway in the furnace room, we did not go up it through the house to get outside. By going down a side street it was not a long walk to the Biology and Chemistry buildings.

Most of my new classmates were planning to go to medical or dental school and were in process of applying to be admitted at the end of their junior year when they would have enough of the required credits for admission. AC and another classmate, Fred Cornet, were going to dental school at the University of Richmond. Because a lot of my class credits were electives in the Engineering Department, I would not have the admission-required courses to enter medical school until the end of my senior year when I would get a BS degree in Biology.

I liked my life as a civilian student, and I liked my academic courses in Biology and Chemistry. My roommate was more of an extrovert and socialite than me. On weekends, he would usually spend some time at the *Bloody Bucket*, a beer-serving restaurant on the edge of town that also sold bottled wine. Sometimes he came in late and drunk to the point of vomiting. A few times he would bring a girl with him to have sex in his bed. He found a regular girlfriend, Alice Alls, in Blacksburg that came to our room frequently to have sex with him. Despite of or because of these weekend socials and lack of studying much he made good grades.

My first quarter as a Junior was good, and I made grades averaging B and good enough to meet medical school admission requirements. General Biology and Chemistry were interesting and having had good training at Hargrave helped me get good grades. There were two or three girls in some of my classes. They were taking Home Economics and, except for one, lived in the Hillcrest Women's Dormitory, *"Skirt Barn"*. Laura Lucas was the daughter of my Chemistry professor and lived with him and her family in a faculty house on campus. She had a quiet demeanor and we talked some between Classes. She accepted my invitation to a dance at the Squires Student Center. I knew the square step with some variations so we did fairly well. I was a perfect gentleman and somewhat naturally nervous, but a little more so to be with the daughter of my Chemistry professor. AC was there and the life of the party. With a few drinks his performance in jitterbug made everyone stop dancing and watch. During one dance with a partner who was equally talented, the twirling and dipping were especially frenetic. In one of the twirling moves, he missed catching her hand and she fell. She was so mad you could almost see the smoke pouring from her hair as she left the dance floor.

Civilian and Biology Student

My second quarter had more advanced Biology and Chemistry classes including Analytical Chemistry, Organic Chemistry, Anatomy and Genetics. My Analytical Chemistry teacher was the head of the Chemistry Department, Dr. Wilbur Watson, and brother of Uncle Fletcher. He knew who I was and my family in Chatham, but he only acknowledged it once in an off-handed way. At the beginning of each class period, he gave a quiz about his study assignment or the previous class. He was known as "Quiz Watson." Organic Chemistry included a Laboratory class where we did various experiments, the last of which was to make pure acetylsalicylic acid (aspirin). Anatomy also had a Laboratory class where we dissected formaldehyde-preserved earth worms and frogs. My Genetics teacher was the Dean of Agriculture, Professor Price, and I think he only taught Genetics I and Genetics II. He was not a demanding teacher and generally followed the text book. The rumor was that during a financially stressful time for VPI, he had used the drill field to grow a bumper crop of tomatoes that brought in enough money to satisfy the college debt. He was made Dean and was kept as Professor with limited academic teaching.

LJ's girl from Pearisburg was in nursing school at Lewis Gale Hospital in Roanoke and said she would find dates for AC and me if we came to Roanoke. We made reservations for two joining rooms at the Jefferson Hotel not far from the nursing dormitory. On Saturday, we rode the bus to Roanoke, checked into the hotel and met the girls at their dormitory. We took them to dinner and then they went to the hotel with us. We took a couple of drinks of whiskey that AC had brought and talked and laughed a lot before my girl and I went into the next-door room. We

172

hugged and kissed a little before returning to the group. AC and his girl then went next door and stayed longer than I had before they returned. His girl lay on the bed and passed out. Her dress was up to her thy and she did not have her panties on. I had a good look at her genital. I wondered what it would be like to have sex with her then, but I did not make any move to find out. LJ and his date stayed in the room and talked and did not go into the other room. AC and my girl then went next door and stayed a long time before returning. By then it was getting close to curfew time for the girls, so we walked with them back to their dormitory. My girl and I held hands along the way, and she bumped her hip against me as we talked and laughed. We kissed and said, "Goodnight."

Slim had decided that he needed a college degree to advance from a journeyman electrician to an electrical engineer. The end of August he came to our room to talk before registering for classes and looking for a room. AC and I were getting three meals daily on a weekly rate next door at Mrs. Tutwiler's boarding house. Slim decided to eat their too, and he found a place to room. Because he had a Model A Ford, he did not need to stay within walking distance to classes.

The third quarter would be the last for most of my classmates as they would volunteer for one of the military services and go to medical or dental school paid for by the branch they entered. AC had been accepted by the dental school at the University of Richmond and had also been accepted by the Navy. Our Genetics II class started normally with Dean Price following the text book for several weeks and then shifting to what we had in Genetics I. At first we students did not understand the shift, and when we did no one had the courage to tell him. After three or four weeks, Dean Price announced that he had gotten his classes confused and put us back on the right text.

In September, 1943 I started my third quarter as a Junior and that is the quarter we had a Senior Prom and received our class rings. The only girl I had dated was Jacqueline, and I liked her too. AC invited a local girl, but since LJ's girl was in nursing school at Lewis Gale Hospital in Roanoke and could not come to the dance. I invited Jacqueline and asked if her friend Catherine Reynolds would come as LJ's date. All was set, and I rented a room in Blacksburg for Jacqueline and Catherine. Etiquette did not allow us to pay for their room, but we did take them to meals and paid other expenses. At the Student Center, Jacqueline and I had our picture taken. She was very pretty in her evening gown with the corsage I had given her. She had blue-violet eyes and black hair, was tall and thin and very pleasant to be with. LJ and Catherine got along well too. I did not dance well, but I was excited to touch and hold Jacqueline as we moved around the floor. We talked some as we danced, and she told me that after I had left from our date at her grandmother's house, she had wrapped a towel around a couple of bricks she had heated in the stove and, after putting them in the foot of her bed to keep her feet warm, the bed clothing caught fire. She was still awake and put the fire out before much damage was done. I was not in a situation that I could offer any kind of relationship, and I did not want a hi-and-goodbye one. At the bus, I kissed her good bye and thanked her for coming and told her I enjoyed her company.

Shortly after the Senior Prom, LJ's mother committed suicide by shooting herself with her 22-cal. pistol. Her arthritis pain was more than she could continue to live with. I had a strange feeling from knowing that I had recently shot the pistol she used to commit suicide. LJ went home and did not return to college while I was there.

The second quarter of Anatomy was a study of a cat's anatomy. During the war, some preserved animals were not available from laboratory supply companies. Cats was one of them. Dr. Hatch, the instructor said that we would have to supply our own specimen. The late-night cat hunt by us anatomy students was on! By calling and giving food my dissecting partners, Dwight & Fred, and I captured a cat and caged it in a cardboard box. The next morning, we took it to Dr. Hatch's laboratory where it was preserved in formaldehyde. We thought we had captured a stray, but a few days later in class, Dr. Hatch said that a lady friend said that her cat was missing. I did not feel good about it, but I needed credit for the Anatomy class. We had not done an efficient job of preserving with the formaldehyde, but the cadaver lasted long enough for us to tease out enough of the anatomical features, organs, nerves and vessels to get credit for the class.

I was originally in the class of 1945, but with year-round attendance I would graduate in September, 1944. I ordered my class ring with my name engraved inside the band, the 1944 date and a garnet stone. The class mates in Pre-Med were getting their grades early before exams to secure their acceptances into medical and dental schools. AC was busy packing his things, and since I was going to the Biology building, he asked me to get his report card filled in for his Genetics II grade. He had been spending time in a beer joint with the teacher, Dean Price, and expected an A. When I gave Dean Price AC's card, he said, " He is a good student, but I think he does not study enough, so I am giving him a C." Probably one of the few college C's AC received and he was in disbelief when I gave him his card.

I stayed in school and took my exams before going home for Christmas vacation. I was the only one of us children at home for the holidays. Paul volunteered for the Army Air Corps at the end of his junior year in 1942 and went to Miami for pilot training. During basic training, a physical examination revealed that he did not have a left ear drum. During his many childhood ear infections, his ear drums had been pierced to drain the infection fluids and the left one had not healed. He was found unfit for pilot training and was sent to Colorado for gunnery maintenance training. Katie had stopped working at Dan River mills and had an office job in Chatham with the Department of Transportation. She lived in a rented room at AC's parents and just came home for Christmas day.

Mother asked me to kill the turkey gobbler that was fattening in a coop. I did, but I partially "botched" the job. The long-time tried and effective method of killing a big turkey for home consumption was to first, hang the turkey by its legs so when the head was severed, all the blood would be drained, second tie the wings closely and securely to the body so the flapping would not break the wings and thus present a desirable wing-tucked appearance on the table. I did not tie the wings securely enough to prevent breaking one wing. Mother made do to still have a nice looking and delicious bird.

It was cold at Windcrest and some rain had frozen and covered the ground with ice. Tuffy still was MY dog, and he was showing his pleasure at having me home by running and jumping around me. I was breaking the ice on the mule watering tub in the stable lot, and Tuffy was running, growling and nipping at the mules' hooves when he slipped on the ice and the mule kicked him in his head. Tuffy lay still, then shaking before laying still again. His skull had been broken. I went to the house and got our 22-cal. rifle and returned. It was too late for Tuffy to recover, so I shot him in his head and took his body below the stable and buried him. Mother and Daddy did not question my judgment and action, nor did I, but it was a sad loss of a good friend.

When I returned to school after Christmas, I was a senior. I did not have a roommate, so I offered to share my room with Slim. He accepted and moved in. Because of the accelerated year-round school schedule and because of the low enrollment, classes of some advanced subjects were only offered once or twice each calendar year. If I did not take a class when it was offered, I would have to wait another year before it would be offered again. To make sure I would graduate on schedule, I started taking 20 to 21 quarter-hours instead of the usual 15 to 18 hours. One of the Biology degree requirements was three quarters of either German or French as a foreign language. German was very difficult for me, and the teacher did not help much either. He may have been legally blind. He wore very thick-lensed glasses and held the text book at nose-distance to read. I had the lowest grades for those two quarters than any I had received. I took one quarter of French for my third quarter requirement. Economics and Psychology were two other non-science courses that I did not easily understand, but I managed to make B's in them.

AC's girl, Alice, came to our room and seemed to like me a little.

She would hug and kiss me and agreed to have a date with me. Slim encourage me and gave me a rubber and instructions on how to use it. I guess he thought I knew everything else that I needed to know. He loaned me his car, and I picked Alice up at her north Blacksburg home. After eating at a convenience/snack bar, we drove to the Blacksburg golf course and parked near some trees. We hugged and kissed some and decided to get in the back seat to have more room. She took her panties off and lay back along the back seat while I put the rubber on. I was as "nervous as a dog shitting razor blades", but I did have a good erection. From there on I sort of guessed my next approach, but Alice helped by guiding my penis into her genital. I waited for the earth to tremble and lightning to strike, but nothing except a little thrill as my penis slid in. She waited a little before I gave up and took my penis out and took the rubber off. We got back in the front seat. I asked if I could try again, and she said, "No", so I took her home. A few days later she went to Richmond to be with AC.

Chapter 11

4F and College End

Virtue is a polite word for fear

Heywood C. Broun

Getting to classes and keeping up with my studies was hard work, and there was little time for a social life. Slim started dating some of the Skirt Barn girls. One was Janette Copenhaver, and she invited Slim and me to visit her in Rural Retreat. She had a younger sister, Lovetta, who was a high-school senior. It was within driving distance from Blacksburg so we got there one Saturday before lunch. We went to a luncheonette not far from their house and danced to jukebox music after we ate. Lovetta was much prettier than Janette, and we got along well. She was dating a senior in her class who came to the luncheonette after we had eaten and joined us in dancing and talking. He was joining his father in dairy farming and already owned a few cows of his own. Lovetta seemed to like him. Slim and I took the girls home and started on our way back to Blacksburg.

Slim was experienced and knew how to get girls interested in him. He grew up on a farm near the all-female Farmville State Teacher's college where he said he had sexual encounters with some of the girls. He was 10 years older than me and most other college students, had been in the Army in the Philippians under General MacArthur, in the Merchant Marines and had traveled around as an electrician journeyman, but he went too far when he had sex with Bessie, a clerk in the nearby drug store. She was older then the college students, overweight and not very good looking. He decided to break off the relationship, but she did not want too. Slim kept avoiding her, and she kept searching for him. When

179

he came into our room he started locking the outside door because he suspected she had been there. One night after dark and after our lights were off, there came a loud knocking and banging on the door. Then Bessie shouted, "Open up this door. I know you are in there. Please let me in." Slim and I were as quiet as church mice until finally she left crying. The next day, Mrs. Johnson told us that she would not tolerate that kind of behavior and for us to not let it happen again. Slim explained to Bessie our situation and told her that if she created another disturbance, he would have her arrested.

Slim started a relationship with a coed, Rudy Elmore, at the skirt barn. Unlike AC, he did not bring her to our room. He and Rudy planned a picnic for them, me and another coed, Texas, who was from Texas and tall, blond and blue-eyed. We went west of Blacksburg about 15 miles and turned onto a winding road up a mountain. He parked the car alongside the road near Mountain Lake, and we walked up a path to near the top of the mountain overlooking the lake and hotel. It was cold and windy, so we were glad that there was no plan to cook anything. The scenic view was beautiful, and the limestone had fossils of sea shells and some other crustaceans as evidence that at one time it had been under the ocean. Also, the girls were nice and friendly. Texas and I wrapped in a blanket on the lea side of a boulder and hugged and kissed some and laughed and giggled as we touched and talked. Slim and Rudy went exploring somewhere for a while, and then we started back to Blacksburg.

Going down the winding mountain road, Slim noticed we were nearly out of gas. Fortunately, there was a convenience store at the intersection of the mountain road and the main highway to Blacksburg. Even though he did not have any gas ration stamps, Slim went in to try to buy some gas hoping the owner would sell him enough to get us home. No luck on that, but he did agree to sell him some kerosene. Slim poured the kerosene into the gas tank, and because there was still gas in the gas line and carburetor the motor started right up. We drove off toward Blacksburg. When the kerosene made it into the motor, it coughed and sputtered a little and blew black smoke out of the exhaust pipe, but it ran well enough at reduced power to make it to let the girls off at Hillcrest dormitory and then to a parking place behind our house. The next day even after putting gas in the carburetor, it would not fire up until Slim had completely replaced the kerosene with gasoline and put in new spark plugs.

On my way walking to class, I met Captain Cheff who called to me. I was surprised to see him and asked if he was visiting someone at VPI. He said that he had stopped teaching at Hargrave to start working at the Celanese plastic plant a few miles west of Blacksburg. He and his wife were staying with her parents on that street until they could get a house near the plant. It was an unexpected pleasure to talk with him and a surprise that he recognized me.

I continued working hard with my studies without much time for entertainment, but Slim continued his relationship with Rudy. I was awakened from a sound sleep by Slim shaking me and asking me to help him get his car. He said that he and Rudy had been riding around the athletic field in the dark with no lights on and he drove over the edge of the field down a steep bank into the tall chain-link fence. The grass-covered bank was too steep to back up, and he did not want his car to be found there at daybreak. He and I got some tools, including bolt cutters and walked to the outside of the fence where his car was. It had run into the wire between two tall steel supporting posts and was sitting straight into the fence. His plan was to cut the wire from top to bottom in front of the car and let it roll through. Regular wire cutters were not strong enough to cut the extra-thick wire, but the bolt cutters were. Dormitories were not far away, so we worked quietly. When the car was free and rolled through, we put the tools and anything else that might be evidence into the car and started quietly pushing it into the road around the drill field. One of us pushed from behind and the other from the driver's side within reach of the steering wheel. There were street lights along the road, but no traffic or pedestrians. The Model A was not a heavy car, but it took a lot of effort to get it past the drill field and campus. We finally felt far enough away from the scene to start the motor and ride the rest of the way home. We did not go near the cut fence for a long time to keep from being seen showing interest in the cut fence.

During spring break, Slim invited me to go to Pamplin to visit his family. In further discussion, we decided that we would spend the night at Windcrest on our way. We stopped at the Hub in Rocky Mount for lunch and then went on to Windcrest. Mother, Daddy and Katie, who was spending the weekend at home, were glad to see us. We had a good time talking, and Slim and Katie joked about the huge difference in their heights. Katie was 5'2", and Slim was 6'3". After breakfast Sunday morning and a few photographs, Slim and I continued toward Pamplin. We stopped in Chatham, and I saw Dr. Anderson on the street outside of

Whitehead's Pharmacy. During our conversation, he said that he could request a health deferment because of my asthma. I told him that I did not want him to do that, but I did not take time to tell him that I wanted to be drafted into the military so I could get my medical school education paid for by the Army. We were about 20 miles from reaching Pamplin when a loud thumping sound came from the right rear fender. The noise got louder, and the car was shaking when Slim pulled over and stopped. One section of the recap on that tire had come loose from the tire and was being slung against the fender and then the road at each rotation. With the repeated impacts, the loose part of the recap had broken in two. We had stopped alongside an old rusty barbed wire fence. Slim had his electrician tools on the back floor-board and used his heavy-duty wire cutters to cut about three or four feet of rusty wire from the fence. After tying two sections of the loose recap securely around the tire and the wheel rim, Slim cut another piece of wire to take with us in case we might need it. We made it on across the railroad tracks into Pamplin and to a garage. Slim knew the people there who traded another recap for his without requiring a ration stamp.

His family welcomed us and made me feel very comfortable being with them. Slim had two sisters living at home. They both were a lot older than me, and they very much favored Slim in looks. We had a good country supper and some conversations afterward. His Daddy was a jolly, plain, good-old-country boy with no pretense. After a good night's sleep and breakfast, it was toilet time. They had a well near their house, but no indoor plumbing. There was an outdoor privy for the women and a log laying behind the stable for the men. On the way to the log, Slim stopped at a shed with corn cobs and brought a big handful with him. We disrobed our behinds and sat across the log for defecation onto the ground behind us. I did not do well in situations like this, but I made it to where I needed a corn cob. This experience was the origination of, "Rough as a cob", and as Slim said, "You want to use white cobs instead of red ones so you can tell if you are bleeding." We made it back to Blacksburg in time for our classes.

My last quarter as an undergraduate kept me busy with my studies. I was into my second quarter of Biochemistry and Pathogenic Bacteriology so I would not have the usual three quarters in those subjects. Going to school year-round and taking extra courses had increased my credit hours enough that I would graduate in June instead of September, 1944, 20 years old and 2years, nine months from when I started. I notified the draft board in Chatham that I would no longer be eligible for an educational deferment after May 15th, and May 20th was set for me to report to Chatham for transport to Roanoke for my army physical and induction into the army.

There were very few of my original classmates left in college, and only three or four who would receive their Biology BS degree with me. A few days before the graduation ceremony, Dougan and I decided to replace the Virginia State flag on one of the flag poles in front of Burruss Hall with our class numerals, 44, painted on a white bed sheet. At around mid-night we took our "flag" to the flag pole where the hoisting ropes were empty. We attached our banner to the snaps, cut the rope just below the attached flag so it could not be used to pull it down and pulled our flag to the top. We secured the rope to hold it up and quickly went home.

The next day our primitive display was our brief declaration of achievement. Not long after noon, the Virginia flag was back in place.

I got good grades on my classes and received my BS degree in Biology at a short ceremony in Burruss Hall. I told Slim and a few other people goodbye and rode the bus home to Windcrest. A couple of mornings later Mother took me to the court house in Chatham. There were about 20 other recruits there waiting for a school bus to take us to Roanoke for physicals and after that we would be sent to a military base for basic training. I told Mother goodbye and promised to write as soon as I arrived at my base. We boarded the bus, and as we pulled away we waved to our families who waved back. People along North Main Street also waved as we passed. I sat next to Charles Viccellio who lived in Chatham. I had not known him, but I knew his twin sisters, and we both knew a lot of the same people in and around Chatham.

At the medical examination clinic, we all stripped and formed a line to move to the examining physicians. We were measured, listened to, tapped and thumped and questioned about our medical history. I was doing alright with the physical examination part, and also with the questions up to the history of asthma question. I did not know how to lie effectively so I answered that I had previously had some asthma attacks, but that I had not had any for three or four years. Too late. The red flag had been thrown. I tried to convince the physician that I was over my susceptibility to asthma, but he said that he did not want to take the chance that in some critical situation in the army I might become incapacitated. There was no other man with me on my return to Chatham.

I do not know the procedure that was used to classify a draftee. I

185

think the results of my physical were referred to my draft board for confirmation and classification. I think that to be sure that my statement about asthma was true, the draft board asked my physician, Cousin Dr. John Anderson. I was classified 4F as physically unfit for military service.

No paid medical education for me, but I was still accepted for enrollment into the medical college of the University of Virginia. I went to Charlottesville and saw my friend and former classmate from VPI, Dwight Whitt, who was going to medical school there in the army physician educational program. He had found a room for me where, like the one I had in Blacksburg, I could fire a furnace in return for rent payment. I then went to the medical college administration building to enroll. My acceptance was approved and then the Department Head told me that my medical college classes would not start until September. During the summer I would take some premedical classes until my regular medical classes would begin. This interim program was designed to let students subject to the draft get an educational deferment until the regular medical school program would start in September. To enroll in this summer session, I would have to pay tuition and buy books. Graduate students at VPI were not charged tuition, and I already had books for my two unfinished subjects of Pathogenic Bacteriology and Biochemistry. To save the money I had, I decided to return to VPI, my free room with Slim and finish the final quarters of my two classes and return to medical school in September.

Slim had not arranged for anyone to share his room and welcomed me back. I enrolled as a graduate student in my two unfinished courses and started class.

Lou had repaid my loan to her with interest, and I needed a car. I wanted a Model A Ford because they were easy to work on and did not have complicated parts. The newspaper ads did not include any and neither did the used car lots that I looked in. All cars were over-priced because of their scarcity. I finally found a black '37 4-door Dodge V8 that seemed in good condition, but I would have to pay $2,000. I bought it and got some gasoline ration stamps. My occupation as a "student" did not qualify me for many per month.

After buying my car and paying for its upkeep, I needed to get some income to keep up with my living expenses. Slim had a job to upgrade the wiring in an old house on the outskirts of Blacksburg and asked me to help. The pay was acceptable, and the experience would be good for me. Slim arranged the work hours to not interfere with our class schedules, and we started work on the house. The job was mainly to add outlets and upgrade the fuse box and some of the old wires. To get wires to the new outlet locations without tearing out the wall between them, we had to take out the baseboards and run the wires through the studs near the floor where they would be hidden when the baseboard was replaced. It was not easy to work in limited space, and special care had to be taken to not damage the baseboard. Slim did the fuse box replacement, and I did most of the outlet additions. The job only took a little more than a week, and I appreciated the pay.

There was a request for VPI students to have blind dates to attend a dance at Radford College. I responded and was given information about where to meet my date, Louise Simmons. I drove to the ballroom where I found her. She was a small girl with brown hair and eyes and average looks. She, like anyone else, could dance better than I, but we had an enjoyable time moving around the dance floor and learning a little about each other. She was a Junior at Radford, and her father was a faculty member living on campus in faculty housing. When I took her home, she accepted my invitation to see her again and go to a movie in Radford. The next week, I picked her up at her house and met her parents. They were very friendly and invited me to spend the night at their house rather than my going back to Blacksburg. I declined, and Louise and I enjoyed being together at the movie after which I kissed her goodnight and left. My life was very unsettled and I did not want to make any close relationships, so I did not contact her again.

One of the professors in the Agriculture Department who was married to a Fitzgerald lady from Chatham, offered me a job to do some yard work at his house on South Main Street. One Saturday I helped him clean gutters, plant some shrubs and rake leaves. It was not much work or pay, but I was glad to have the association with Chatham natives.

Later in the summer, Slim got another job. This one was with the town to survey and plot the locations of graves in the old part of the Blacksburg Cemetery. He found his rod-and-tape helper in me. Many of the old grave sites were barely visible, and some of the headstones were degraded so that the inscriptions were illegible. We could clean and increase the quality of some of the inscription enough to read some of the names and dates. Slim set up and did the transit work, and I placed and held the pole. We both did the tape measurements. Slim did all the data recording and map preparation for the town.

4F and College End

A former classmate, Brad, whom I did not know very well came back to the campus while on leave from the Merchant Marines. One evening we decided to go to the Bloody Bucket and get a steak dinner. On the way out of town, there were two girls hitchhiking. I pulled over and Brad asked where they were going. One said, "Christiansburg." He said for them to get in. One of the girls said her name was Helen Shiflet. I did not understand what the other girl said. They agreed to have supper with us at the Bloody Bucket. We talked some while we were eating and found that the girls lived in the country not far from Christiansburg. Both had finished high school and were working part-time at a grocery store. On our way to taking the girls home, we stopped in the parking lot of the closed store where they worked. I got in the back seat with Helen, and the other girl got in the front seat with Brad. There was some serious hugging and kissing between Helen and me. I wasn't paying attention to what Brad and his girl were doing. After a little while, I told Brad to drive and take the girls home. We went up a winding road and pulled into the driveway and stopped a little distance from Helen's house. I asked Helen what her father did for a living, and she said he was a preacher. I opened the door and got out, but Helen just lay down on the seat with her lower legs hanging from the outside edge of the seat and looked at me with a smile and outstretched arms. In the subliminal part of my brain I was thinking; I did not have a rubber; we were in her driveway not very far from her house; her father was a preacher and likely to come out at any second with a shotgun in his hands. All of my lust of the moment disappeared into a wisp of past tense. I took Helen's hands and pulled her up and kissed her good night, and got in the driver's seat and drove off.

I was more than half way through the summer quarter and found that it would be a struggle to have enough money to stay in graduate school at VPI, and it would be impossible for me to work enough and pay expenses to go to medical school. My friend Marse Ferrell had joined the Merchant Marines and was sailing Kaiser Liberty ships in convoys to Murmansk, Russia. That might be a way for me to serve in the war effort and maybe go to medical school when the war was over. I asked Brad where I would go to enlist in the Merchant marines. He said there was an enlistment station in the Flat Iron Building on the docks in Norfolk, and they would take anybody that had a heartbeat. The next time I had a day without classes, I drove to Norfolk and found the recruiting office. During the application process when I was asked about my draft status, I told them I was classified 4F because of mild asthma. I explained that I had not had any problems during the past 3 years and was sure there would be no cause for a recurrence on the ocean. I did have a heartbeat, and I was in good health. I was rejected again. I returned to classes and to the part-time job I had in the Agronomy analytical lab. I analyzed hay samples for nitrogen, phosphorus and potassium (NPK).

One of the faculty in the lab, James Roberts, said that he had a niece visiting him and invited me to come one evening to visit his family and to meet Evelyn Phipps. After supper when I got to his house, he his wife and Evelyn greeted me with some drinks and snacks. James and his family were from near Wythville, and Evelyn was looking for a job to be on her own. James and his wife said, "Good night." and went upstairs. Evelyn had long, coal-black hair, dark brown eyes and a ruddy complexion. She was not a beauty, but was very nice looking. We talked some about me and what I was doing, and we talked about her plans to seek employment in Roanoke. She responded when I hugged and kissed her, and she did not resist when I rubbed my hand on her breast and along her legs. I pulled her dress up, and she lay on the couch waiting. There must be a more powerful word for "nervous" to describe my feelings. Her uncle and aunt were just up a few steps in a very small house. My penis was like a limp scrap of cloth, and as hard as I tried, I could not even get it up enough to get the rubber on. I asked Evelyn if we could go outside, but she refused. I apologized, said I would like to see her again and left. Forced marriages were not uncommon, and I did not want to be part of one of them.

Another decision time for me. If I stayed where I was, I had a part-time job, free room, free tuition, a few graduate credits and a little money. I decided to explore the possibility of getting a Master's degree in Bacteriology with my teacher, Dr. Orcutt, as adviser. He said that he would be glad to have me and that he could get me financial aid for preparing media and other lab work for his undergraduate classes. When I quit my work with the Agronomy Department, James said that Evelyn had a job with a bank in Roanoke.

I was getting along well in my class work, and the lab work for Dr. Orcutt required me to prepare petri dishes with a gel bacteria-growing media and test tubes with liquid media. I also did some of the incubation of samples and a lot of lab-ware washing and sterilizing. I had one class, Comparative Anatomy, taught by Dr. Hatch, my undergraduate anatomy teacher. He paid me to help him in some of his private Veterinarian work.

He had a female cat in his lab that he was going to spay for a lady in town. As we were taking her out of her cage, she got loose and became very upset, and ran around the lab and under furniture. Her shrieking, and spitting with bared teeth and striking exposed claws were a challenge. The gauntlet gloves that I was wearing saved me from serious injury while I was trying to catch her. I held her on the operating table while Dr. Hatch injected the anesthetic. Watching him remove the two ovaries through a button-hole incision in her abdomen was fascinating for me. He knew exactly where to catch the fallopian tubes with his hooked instrument and pull it out to excise them. He put in a couple of stitches, put on disinfectant and secured a bandage before we put her in a recovery cage.

There was a commercial fox farm near Christiansburg that he monitored and treated ill or cut animals. The red, silver and gray foxes were kept in outdoor fenced cages attached to all-weather houses. The houses of these cages were on both sides of a walkway. When I went with Dr. Hatch, he did not need to treat any of the foxes. There were also several cages with mink at this farm. On our way back to Blacksburg, we stopped for him to treat a horse with an infected front leg.

Dr. Orcutt did not say anything about paying me, so I asked him when I would be paid for my lab work. He said that the money he thought he would get from the college was not available. I told him I would have to quit the lab work and get another job or get credit for the work. He became very upset and said that he expected me to continue without pay or credit. He was so emotional that I could not reason with him. Then he became verbally abusive and said that if I tried to continue education in the Biology Department he would block any attempt I made to get a degree.

I went to Dr. Hatch's office and told him that I had a disagreement with Dr. Orcutt and that I would be leaving school. He said that he would be my adviser so that I could stay. I then told him what Dr. Orcutt said about refusing his approval during my oral exams for an advanced degree in the Biology Department. I could not take that risk by continuing to get the required academic credits and then be turned down for a degree by flunking my oral examination by heads of departments in the Biology Department. I thanked him and left. I had made a bad choice of advisers and wished I had chosen differently.

Chapter 12
Teaching, Courting and Marriage

Education is identical with helping the child realize his potentialities.

Erich Fromm

I went home in November 1944 before Thanksgiving with no job or prospect of getting one and no plans for my future.

Daddy had been passed over for a promotion in favor of another person with a more impressive education. He was embarrassed and did not want to stay and work under those conditions. He came home to live and help mother with the chickens and garden. There was no local job that would give the same prestige, so he accepted a position as a board member of Planters Bank and told people he had retired from The Federal Land Bank which was mostly true even though he did not have enough employment time or age until later. He also became very active in Greenpond Baptist Church.

He did have a plan. He ran as a candidate for the Board of Directors of the Federal Land Bank in the district we were living in. The sitting member was unhappy and tried to get Daddy to withdraw, but Daddy persisted.

I tried to help Daddy with some of his work, but he did not need my help so I mostly just stayed in the log cabin and ate meals with my parents. I went to church with them and got a date with Katherine Reynolds, who had been a date for my roommate, LJ, at our junior prom at VPI. She was a very pretty blond girl with big blue eyes and a couple of years younger than me who lived a short distance away. Our date at her home went well, and I planned to see her again. In our community every event was news to be spread as fast and far as possible, so when I was at

the local general store a few days later I was told that Katherine was Ted Anderson's girlfriend. Ted was in the army doing his duty and I was at home doing nothing, so I did not date Katherine anymore.

I found out that Jacqueline had a job at the Hughes Orphan School in Danville and visited her Uncle Ben and Aunt Ella Anderson at Climax on some weekends. I made a date with her to see her at Ben's house. When Billy Bowen died, his property had been divided among his 15 children, and the old store was sold to my second cousin, Ben Anderson. Ben built a small filling-station/beer and wine store and a very small two-story house on the corner lot. It was nice to see Jacqueline again and also to see Ben and Ella. After talking some, Ben and Ella went up the steep stairs to their bedroom. This seemed a replay of the embarrassing situation I had with Evelyn, so I made no intimate advances with Jacqueline. We just talked and hugged and kissed some. I found she had been a teacher's aide at Climax while she was waiting to get her job at Hughes.

By Christmas Daddy had decided to find a job for me and told me to contact a friend of his, Colonel Aubrey H. Camden, the president of Hargrave, about a job there. I did and was given a "made-up" job to research and organize old school records. I was given $100/month plus room and board to start January 3, 1945. My room was in a Hargrave-owned house joining the main campus where I was also house faculty supervisor of the few students who lived there. I had my meals with the rest of the faculty and students in the mess hall. I was given an office and access to student records to work on. Captain Brooks had been promoted to Major and welcomed me as a new faculty member and said he remembered how smart I was in his classes. Shocked! I said that he must have me confused with my brother Paul, but he insisted it was I. Paul and I have widely different personalities so I rethought his comments and wondered how I could have impressed then Captain brooks instead of Paul. I did not know anything about Paul's time at Hargrave, so to have Major Brooks welcome me in such a way caused me to wonder what his experiences there had been.

I did not work on student records long until I was assigned to teach a group of special (incorrigible) 8th graders, who had been taken from regular classes to prevent them from disrupting the education of other students. They were being supervised by Mr. Norman Childs who was about 45 and on the verge of a nervous breakdown. He had become so frustrated that when there was disorder, he would grab the first pupil he could and shake him, shout angrily at him and vigorously shove him back into his seat. I was 21 just out of college and available to try dealing with the antics of that class. I don't know what happened to Mr. Childs, but I think he was given the record-searching job.

I shared the teaching of these cadets with Coach William French who had them in the afternoons, and I had them in the mornings. There were about 10 cadets in this class, and I wanted to have them learn academically as well as discipline. In my first session with them I explained that I expected orderly conduct, but if there was disorder, I would punish the offender with reasonable strikes of a belt to his buttock. Each additional offense would be dealt with a little more forcible punishment. To be fair, I would not punish anyone if I could not determine who the offender was.

While my rules appeared logical to me, they did not have any effect on this group of irresponsible and incorrigible children. Each time I turned my back to illustrate something on the chalk board, some disturbance would happen. I followed my rules, but there was no improvement among the pupils. One of the senior students, sympathetic with my situation with the class, loaned his fraternity paddle to me. Even this additional level of punishment had little effect. The boys were not mean in an aggressive way. They were just mischievous and unruly, thus keeping me constantly alert as a care taker rather than as a teacher. My other work was as assistant athletic coach under Coach French.

Word of my method of discipline reached the administrative office, and I was called in for a meeting with Col. Camden. He said that he had heard that I was using physical methods of discipline on the students in my class and that was not allowed to be used anymore. I told him that what I was doing was the "normal" method of punishment that had been used during my school years and did not realize that it was no longer approved. I started using the demerit system that did not improve discipline either.

I gave the paddle to Coach French who "taught" the class in a second-floor room of the athletic building where there were desks with chairs and some stored athletic equipment. The discipline problem could not be separated from the group and traveled with them. One boy sitting on the back row of desks put on a football helmet and attracted the rest of the class with antics. Coach French had the offender come to the front of the room and bend over to receive a strike from the paddle. Coach French gave a vigorous blow, and the paddle split right down the middle with a thud. The boy had put a large bolt in his back pocket. That ended physical punishment by Coach French and reinstated the demerit-only system for him too.

In addition to the special 8th grade students, I became Assistant Coach for varsity basketball and coached the junior and interscholastic basketball teams. My attempt to have each dormitory hall form a team and compete against each other was not successful, and my assistant coaching was mostly during home and away games. I did not have much to do at home games except have the supplies and equipment ready and available.

One of my first away games was a night game at Staunton Military Academy in Staunton, Virginia. Coach French drove the school athletic bus and I drove my car with some athletic gear. We got to Staunton in the afternoon before the game, checked in at the Academy athletic department and unloaded our uniforms and equipment and then checked in at the hotel. Coach French and I shared one room with a large bed, and the athletes had rooms on a different floor. We ate supper and then went to the basketball court and played a close but loosing game. While the boys were getting dressed, Coach French had a friendly conversation with two girl spectators and invited them to come to our hotel room. After loading the bus, we all went to the hotel. Shortly after we were in our room, the two girls knocked on our door and came in. Coach made some drinks for us, and we talked for a little then turned off the lights. With our lights out, one girl lay on the bed with Coach, and the other one and I were in an oversize chair. Coach and his girl were obviously having sex. My girl and I were just hugging and kissing. When they got up and went to the bath room, I asked my girl to get in the bed with me. She said, "No.", and when her friend was dressed, they left. Coach and I went to sleep, and the next morning we went back to Hargrave. I took a route through Roanoke on my way back and called Evelyn at the bank where she worked. It was not long before she would get off, and she said I could come and take her home. I picked her up at the bank and took her to her apartment. We talked some along the way, and she said that she was going with someone. He was expecting her in a little while. We talked some more in her apartment while she freshened up, and I took her to where she said I should let her off so that her boyfriend would not see her get out of my car. We kissed goodbye.

I met a girl at our game at Ferrum College and at another game when we played William Byrd High School in Lynchburg. We wrote a few letters to each other, but they were too far away for me to have as a "girlfriend", so I discontinued my correspondence. I contacted Jacqueline at Hughes school and asked her for a date. She said that she was going to spend the weekend in Gretna with a girlfriend. I agreed to pick her up on Friday at the end of her work and take her to Gretna. On my way to Danville I stopped at Coach French's house, told him I was on my way to pick up a girlfriend and asked if I could borrow some whiskey and a condom. He introduced me to his wife and got a half-full bottle of whiskey and a couple of paper cups that we put in my car. I talked with Mrs. French while he went back inside. When he came out, he slipped a condom to me. I said goodbye and went to get Jacqueline. I was impressed by how pretty Mrs. French was and wondered why someone with a wife that beautiful and nice would be having sex with those pick-up sluts.

Jacqueline and I stopped at a filling station where I bought a cold, large Coca Cola after which I pulled into a side road and parked. She agreed to have a drink with me, so I poured twice as much whiskey in her cup as in mine and added the Coke. At that point I was dying to pee, and I told her so and said I would be back in a minute. I got out, went around to the back of the car and urinated. We drank our whiskey and talked some, and I was feeling the effects of the alcohol. My advances were responded to with, "We need to go to Altavista and get my friend at the store where she works and have supper." I drove on and we got her friend, had another moderate drink with her, had supper and I took them to her friend's house. By that time, I was getting really high. The two girls seemed sober, but did not object when I hugged and kissed her friend and grabbed her behind and did the same with Jacqueline. I left and was trying to stay awake. I pulled into a VDOT gravel storage lot along the side of the road and rested some until I felt I could safely make it to my room at Hargrave. The next day I realized that Jacqueline had switched cups when I got out of the car to pee.

When I asked Jacqueline for another date, she said that she was engaged to marry Rodney Suttle and would not go out with anyone else anymore.

When basketball season was over, Coach French coached baseball and I coached track and field to the end of the school year in June. My experience as manager of track and field under Coach White during my senior year gave me enough knowledge and experience to do well coaching, and some of the athletes performed well enough to place in the top 2 in competition with other private schools.

One afternoon I saw Marian Anderson with some of her school friends at the Whitehead Drugstore soda fountain, and we spoke to each other in a friendly manner. We talked about what we had been doing since we had last seen each other in school at Climax and about her brothers who were in the military. During the end of our conversation when we were leaving I realized that I was still attracted to her. I was too bashful to ask for a date, and I also remembered her earlier slap at Climax so I said, "Maybe I'll see you again sometime." My expectation being that she would be polite and respond with "maybe", but she responded, "When?" That really put me on the spot, so I gave her a date and time. I kept our date and went to see her at her home in the "Woodlawn" suburbs of Chatham. We sat in the parlor for a while and had a nice conversation about what she was doing and what I had been doing since we knew each other seven years previously. She was very nice, and I asked to see her again. I also was looking to find some other girls to date, and made a few attempts with no success.

Marian was active in her English class plays that were being presented to the public. Her English teacher, Mr. Kidd, was also the Presbyterian minister. Some Sunday afternoons he and his two high-school daughters would have a reception and reading at their house for some of the thespian group. I went to one as Marian's date. I don't remember the name of the play that her senior class was practicing for, but when it was performed, it received very favorable comments from the local newspaper and people in the community. Our going together was known by all of her school friends so we were a topic at her graduation and by her Class Historian. Something like, "Marian has Walter on a halter" brought laughter from the audience and a little public embarrassment to me.

In Chatham, I was walking by the Bank of Chatham when Jewel Fox Trent came out and said, "Hi Walter." I was surprised and greeted her with a smile. She was smiling and seemed glad to see me. She was even more beautiful than she was the last time I had seen her, and I was thinking that the judges in the Miss Virginia contest should have chosen Jewel when she competed as Miss Pittsylvania County. We talked a little about me and what I was doing, and then I asked about her. She was staying with her mother at her home near Climax since her husband had been killed during the Normandy D-Day invasion nearly a year ago. She had a little girl named Jewel Lee. She said that she had sworn that she would never name her child for her, but that Gordon had insisted so they compromised by naming her for them both. She was smiling and laughing during our conversation and seemed sincere when she invited me to come to see her. I thanked her, and we parted as she walked away toward her parked car and I continued to Whitehead's Pharmacy. Marian was at the soda fountain with some high-school friends, and we had a coke at the counter before I took her home.

My teaching year at Hargrave was nearly over, and I did not want to continue with the professionally limiting employment. Thus, I obtained a position as math and science teacher at the same school Marian and I had attended, Climax High School, starting in the fall. Marian had been planning to go to college, but later in the summer there had been a change in her plans that did not include college. She continued living at home with her parents and had no plans for her future. I was living in the two-room log cabin summer house on our farm near Climax.

I thought about Jewel and her child, and I thought about Marian. I decided that I wasn't ready to be a father yet, and I had fallen in love with

Marian who loved me too. My previous dreams about Jewel had now been replaced by the love of my life, Marian.

Marian's father, Otha Anderson, had been a tobacco farmer, but with his three sons enlisted in the armed forces he had to quit and sold his farm to buy the house in Woodlawn. He had a war-time job in the Newport News Ship Yard and did not come home often. I only saw him a few times when I visited Marian. Most of my visits were spent sitting in her parlor or in the swing on her porch. Her mother rarely participated in my visits, and I only remember having a few meals there, one when her oldest brother, John, was on furlough for a few days. After the meal, Marian and I went for a ride and came back a little later than originally planned. I did not go in with Marian, but she told me that John was upset by her late return and said, "Mother ought to whip your ass for staying out so late". Sometimes during my visits Marian and I would drive to visit one of her girlfriends and stop at a secluded spot to hug and kiss a little.

One afternoon when I was taking her home from school, we stopped in a secluded spot along a dead-end road and kissed and hugged some. She let me touch her legs under her dress and when I got out she lay on her back across the front seat with her dress up and legs hanging over the edge of the seat. I rubbed her panties with my hand and was unzipping my pants when a young man came walking down the road. I just stood where I was as he walked on by without his seeing Marian. I re-zipped my trousers and told Marian that we should get her home.

Mrs. Anderson was a "stay-at-home" wife and mother, but she bought produce from farmers and home gardeners to resell at the "Curb Market" in Danville. I think one of her cousins was a partner in this as Mrs. Anderson did not drive. At one of the sales, she bought a goat to clear her fenced back lot of bushes and briers. The fence was not much of a challenge for the goat which was soon gone. It was reported to be several miles away at the Norman Dairy farm. Because I had a car and was available, Marian and I went for the goat. It was running wild in plain sight in the barnyard. It would jump up onto a low shed roof then up onto the roof of the main barn to the very top and then come barreling down full speed to the ground again. With help from Halcut Norman and some feed and coaxing, the three of us got it into a stall. With the back windows closed we got her into the back seat of my four-door Dodge. Marian tried to keep the goat calm while I drove to her house. Mrs. Anderson had a chain and collar ready which we put securely around its neck before opening the car door. The goat was retrieved, and only a small amount of my rear seat cushion had been eaten. From this experience, I learned to not like goats.

When my car would need some minor repair, I would take it to Connor Brothers & Sours Garage where AC's father was the owner. The automatic choke was a new feature on the 1937 Dodge, and its performance did not meet expectations and required frequent adjustments. Mr. Jessie Sours usually did the work on my car. On one visit while I was waiting, a mutual friend of AC and me came in. During our conversation, he told me about ACs' experience at dental college. He did not know the girl's name that AC had spent the weekend with at a cabin in the outskirts of Richmond, but AC did not make it back to class in time for a final exam. When the class instructor posted the exam and semester grades, AC received a "B" for both. The other students knew he was not present and objected. The Department Head took over and meted out punishment to the instructor and to AC. Thus, AC was not given credits for the class and had to attend an extra semester to compensate for his lost credits. That was typical of AC.

Marian and I went to a movie at the new movie theater on Pruden Street where we sat on the back row and held hands, and we went to a minstrel show at the Chatham High School auditorium. My cousin, Les Whitehead, was a member of the Chatham Fire Department which sponsored a fund raiser by putting on the show. In their exaggerated charcoal-covered black faces and overly thick painted red lips, their tattered hats and wildly bright-colored patches on their clothes, it was hard to tell who the actors were. I think Les was the Interlocutor sitting in front of a semicircle of the others. The beginning started with Stephen Foster music sung by the group accompanied by tambourine, fiddle and banjo with the Interlocutor exaggeratedly conducting. The troupe would dance around in random, uncoordinated steps and poses to the consternation of the "Conductor." Next came questions and prompts from the Interlocutor. All questions and answers were in mispronounced and indistinct old-slave dialect. Marian and I laughed a lot at the hilarious performance.

My first cousin, Louise Yeatts (Gatewood), had heard that I would be teaching at Climax that fall and invited me for Sunday dinner at her home near Callands. Her son, James, and daughter, Billie Louise, were there too. Her husband, Letcher, was at their convenience store across the highway from their house. We had a big country dinner along with a lot of talking. Louise was retired from thirty years of teaching 4th grade at Callands and gave me some advice from her experience. She said that her strongest and most useful advice was, "For the first two or three weeks you teach, do not smile, and above all else do not let even the slightest unruly thing pass without your taking extremely forceful disciplinary action. After you have established your authority, you can let up a little and still have control."

Marian was the only girl I had ever dated more than once or twice, and she was the only girlfriend that I could call my "Steady" girl. It was a nice feeling to know that she was there and glad for my visits and affection. Our hugs and kisses and feeling her body close to mine was an exciting and overwhelming experience for me that I enjoyed and desired.

We continued to date during the summer and decided to get married. I wanted to buy her a diamond ring but did not have enough money to purchase one that I thought she would like. My parents said that I could use their car to visit Marian if I sold mine, so I sold my 37 Dodge and bought her a 1 carat emerald-cut diamond gold ring that she was proud to wear. She set the date for the day after my Christmas holiday started, December 21, 1945.

Between the time I sold my car and our marriage I visited her using my parent's car some of the times, and I walked and hitchhiked other times. One time I was given a ride by a neighbor, Wright Mitchell, who turned out to be very drunk and reckless. I did get out safely, but wished I had turned down his offer of the ride. I remember walking the 11 miles home in the dark after one visit. There was no moon so I had to watch the star-lit sky and silhouettes of trees and utility poles to stay in the road. It was a long walk home with no traffic that late at night. Original homes in this area were built before electricity was available so they were built near a source of drinking water. Springs were in lower places near creeks while roads were built on ridges where there was good drainage. Thus, most houses were off the road some distance so there was only an occasional dog barking in the distance to break the silence of my journey. My thoughts were only of Marian and what our life together might be. I had no money, just a stable job that offered subsistence living for two. With our mutual love and affection, I did not think very far into the future.

She was a smoker, and cigarettes were of poor quality and in short supply for civilians during the war. I think one brand was "Piedmont", and known as "floor sweepings." I would find cigarettes to take to her and she would smoke while we sat in her swing on the porch. I did not take up that habit.

World War II was finally over, and Paul had come home from his several years of duty in Italy. It was a joy to see him safe and back home again. Mother and daddy treated him like the long-lost son that he was.

Marian and I were living in the cabin, and mother had been doing the milking as usual, but before daylight on the morning after Paul arrived home I heard mother calling, "Walter, Walter, Walter." I finally woke enough to answer, and she shouted back, "Come and get the bucket and go milk the cow." I dressed and went to the house and told mother that I didn't know how to milk the cow and that she or Paul had always milked her. Her response was that Paul had had a hard time in the Army and that he was not going to milk the cow. She said that it was time I learned and to go and milk anyway and do the best I could. I did. I don't think I got all the milk from the udder that I should have, and it was a hard learning process for me. From then on I was the cow milker. A few weeks later Paul went back to the UA to finish getting his degree in Political Science.

My first few days teaching were a time of students testing my disciplinary vulnerability. As Louise had advised me, I gave no quarter with a stern face. In my plain geometry class, a Rigney boy stood up and started to walk. I did not even ask him to sit down. I told him that I did not tolerate misbehavior in my class and to leave the class and stand in the hall until the class was over. He was so surprised and startled he had no time to argue and left as I had instructed. The rest of the students seemed just as surprised and gave me quiet attention. The word must have spread fast because pupils in my other classes did not try to test me. Louise's advice and my use of it seemed to be working.

After we were engaged, my sister, Sallie invited us to visit her in

Newport News where she and her son Paul Reynolds were living while her husband, Arthur Ryan, Jr., was serving in the Navy in the South Pacific. We took the bus in Chatham for a long ride to Newport News where Sallie and Paul met us and took us to the apartment where they lived. Sallie was really happy that we were engaged and showed us her pleasure by introducing us to her other war-widow friends in her apartment complex, and providing tasty food bought using her food ration coupons. At bedtime, she and Paul disappeared into their bedrooms to leave Marian and me alone in the living room. We hugged and kissed a little before she went to the bedroom Sallie provided, and I slept on the sofa.

The next day, Sunday, Marian and I took a city bus to see her father at his room in a boarding house. He just had one room with no common area for visitors in the house. He congratulated us on being engaged, but the conversations were short and forced with not much to talk about between us. He was mild-mannered and shy with us, so we did not stay long.

Monday, with Sallie still bubbling with joy, we left on the long bus journey home. We talked a lot about plans for our future and the happiness we had found in each other.

Because she was 17 and not of legal age to marry, her Mother, Annie Kate, had to go before the county clerk to officially give her consent, which she did. All three of Marian's brothers, John, Sam and Taz were in the military. John and Sam were in the Army and Taz was in the

Navy.

We were married in her parent's house in the late afternoon of December 21, 1945 with just her parents, my parents and the Green Pond Baptist Church preacher, Mr. Harold Baer, attending. After the ceremony and the traditional kisses, wedding cake and punch, we were congratulated with good wishes. Daddy slipped a $20 bill to me, and Marian and I took a taxi to the Danville Hotel where we spent the first night of our married life together. It was a fumbling experience for both of us, but I had learned enough from my one-girl experience to have success for me. I don't think Marian had an orgasm. It did not seem strange to me because I had no idea how women should feel during intercourse.

I grew up on our farm, and of all the breeding animals I watched, the female just seemed passive while the male did all the movements and heavy breathing. Also, periodically our Baptist preacher, Mr. Kessler, would have a sermon on marriage relationships which always included, "Wives, submit to your husband" and this gave me a feeling of guilt and shame about masturbation and sex that I still felt uncomfortable about even after being married.

When we were married, all my dreams of sex came true. A beautiful blonde, blue-eyed lady happily and cooperatively shared my bed. I truly had arrived in paradise. There was no other wish left in my life other to make it last.

Chapter 13

Starting A Path to the Future

It is a principle innate and co-natural to every man to have an insatiable inclination to the truth, and to seek for it as for hid treasure.

Thomas Aikenhead

After our honeymoon in Danville we went to live in the two-room log cabin that I had been staying in alone. There was one room downstairs and a steep stairway going to the bedroom upstairs. The downstairs was used as living room, dining room and kitchen. I had purchased a kerosene-fueled cooking range at the auction of my deceased Aunt Nannie Whitehead's estate. We had a few other pieces of furniture that had been given to us. There was a stone chimney with fireplace which we covered with sheet metal to accept a wood-burning heater. We got water from a faucet outside, and we had an outdoor "Johnnie House". We had no car, but I was allowed to ride the public school bus to and from my teaching job at school. We were allowed to use my parent's car on some occasions, and we used their farm to have a pig and a few chickens. I milked their cow for some of the milk. We had the bare essentials and were living on my salary of $125 per month. Later that spring I bought a much-used black 1930 Ford Model A "turtle-back" coupe.

Aunt Nannie Whitehead had died that fall, and her handwritten will was not signed. Mother said that Uncle Hurt had helped with her will and should have known that for it to be legal it had to be signed. Because Aunt Nannie was not married and did not have children, her nearest blood relatives were asked to agree to accept her will as she had written and not require the court to settle her estate. Uncle Jeb had died so his three children had his right to determine his vote. Mother said that everyone except Uncle Jeb's son, Douglas, agreed to accept Aunt Nannie's will as she wrote it. Douglas blocked a unanimous agreement, so everything in her estate had to be sold. Mother went to the auction and bought a small kerosene-burning cook stove for me, and she said that her brothers and sisters bought the rest to distribute the items according to her will. When I asked about Grandfather's saber and bullet, Mother said that Aunt Nannie had willed them to Grandfather's namesake and oldest grandson, Richard Whitehead. Mother and her siblings were not happy with Douglas for forcing the auction so he could receive a little larger inheritance.

We had only been married a couple of months when Marian was taken very ill with upset stomach and vomiting. I took her to Chatham to the local family physician, Dr. Hammer, who diagnosed her as pregnant. She continued with morning sickness for another month or more and started care from an obstetrician in Danville. Marian's symptoms of pregnancy were a surprise to both of us and a quick learning experience.

Marian's mother and father had some disagreement which brought Marian's mother to stay with us for a few days until Mr. Anderson came and took her home. I learned later that they had frequent quarrels resulting with her leaving to stay with her brother or some other family member. Marian was held hostage by Mr. Anderson some of those times to induce Mrs. Anderson to come back. When things were really bad between them Mrs. Anderson said that he would destroy her best clothes and shoes so that she would be too ashamed to leave. Marian was the youngest child and her mother's true love. As Marian grew up, they became very attached to each other. As a child she was used as the bargaining pawn.

Most of our social life was with family and church. Being a school teacher made me vulnerable and obligated to accept a request to teach the young adult Sunday school class at Greenpond Church where we attended and I was a member. I did this for a couple of years before finding a face-saving reason to quit. I think it was my seven-day dairy work. Also, the church was sponsor of a Boy Scout troop with the pastor, Mr. Baer, as Scout Master. I was chosen to be Assistant Scout Master. I think the sponsorship ended after about a year when Mr. Baer decided to leave the church to become a missionary to some Native American tribe in Arizona.

Some Sunday afternoons Marian and I would drive to local landmarks. On one of these excursions we went to Louis Island Bridge, a covered bridge across Pigg River about six miles from our home. A rope was tied to a limb high in a bank-side tree where as ten- and teen-agers my brother and sister and our Hudson cousins would swing out over the river and fall in as a simulated "cannon ball." A rope still hung from the tree, but we were not interested in using it.

When we were ready to leave, one of the tires on our Model A was flat. That was not uncommon during the shortages of WWII. We had a spare but no jack. Marian's extra weight of pregnancy helped after we found some rocks to use as a fulcrum and a long pole as a lever for her to sit on to lift the car while I changed the wheel.

Later in the early 1950s Louis Island Bridge was washed away during a summer regional flood. Only some of the rock foundation and pilings were left.

Because I was not paid my teachers salary during the three summer months, I measured government-controlled tobacco acreage. I started that first summer measuring tobacco fields east of Chatham so as not to be involved with my immediate neighbors. The method of measurement was by determining distances using a tape with the help of the farmer, making a dimensional diagram and computing areas by using plane geometry. It was not hard work and offered opportunities to meet local farmers. My pay was based on the amount of acreage I measured and the number of farms I served. One of the farms I worked on was Claude and Marguerite Whitehead's. It consisted of two or three separate farms with the home farm being about a thousand acres with a large tobacco allotment. Claude had worked as a buyer for American Tobacco Company in Central America. One of its brands, Chesterfield, was in process of making a movie on their farm about bright-leaf tobacco farming. Their two younger sons, Claude, Junior and Joe, were in the movie which was named, "Bright Leaf", and when it was finished was shown in local movie theaters. Marse was still in the Merchant Marines.

Our first child, Anne Whitehead, was born September 21, 1946. Because we did not trust my model A Ford to get her to the hospital in Danville for delivery, we had an agreement to use my parents more modern car. Of course, her labor pains started at night, and it was an exciting time for both of us. The car overheated on the way to the Danville hospital, so we had to stop for water for the radiator at a closed filling station. Finding an empty container and water took some time which added to our stress.

I was allowed in the delivery room until it was determined the baby was being born. Then I had to go to the waiting room to wait until morning when Anne was born. I think Marian and Anne were in the hospital for three or four days before being discharged. Marian and Anne stayed with her mother for about a week before coming home.

The second year of teaching at Climax I also tried doing some farming. I used my father's mules and farming tools to raise a small plot of corn. Some school days I needed to do farm work. My mother looked after Anne so Marian could take my place at school as substitute teacher so that we would not lose my pay for those days. I think she really enjoyed those experiences, and the students liked having her.

Because the war effort had taken a lot of potential men teachers, there had not been much sports activity. The Agriculture teacher, Arch Yeatts, Jr., had been coaching an intramural baseball team, but inter school games were limited because of gasoline and teacher shortages. My first year teaching at Climax I decided to start a boy's basketball team using students who had never played the sport and knew very little about it. I think the school furnished the ball, and each student supplied his own pair of black shorts, white T-shirt and shoes. It was a good time for the players and parents. There were one or two with talent for the game, but inexperience in ball-handling and lack of developing planned-play strategy prevented us from winning any games that first year. The second year of basketball the boy's team did better, and going to other schools made life more interesting for the players. The girls did not have any sports and wanted a girl's basketball team. There was no woman teacher willing to coach them, so they begged me until I consented. That was when the girl's court was divided into three sections with two girls as forwards to shoot goals, one girl in center court to relay the ball between forwards and the guards at the opposite end of the court from the forwards who tried to block the opposing forwards and to intercept the ball. Because of their and my inexperience, it was a challenging experience for all of us. A few of the girls were really cute making the experience interesting for me.

In 1947, my deceased Great Uncle Charlie Anderson's farm was divided and sold at auction to settle his estate. A 96 acre tract joined my father's farm, and he bought that for, I think, $25/acre and sold it and his lower 65 acre tract to me on credit. This drastically increased my interest in farming and allowed me to start sharing in the Aberdeen Angus beef cattle my parents had in addition to having milk cows and pigs.

Our entertainment was limited because of work requirements and limited income. Marian found a subscription service for vinyl records of popular music that we could afford and enjoy together. We had a spring-wound acoustic Victrola and a few old records that were nearly worn out, so the new popular music of our monthly choice was a refreshing sound.

Marian was interested in art but had no training or experience. She enrolled in a correspondence course in oil painting and really enjoyed her lessons. Each assignment was sent in for criticism and suggestions, and she took the suggestions to apply as she progressed.

Because the war effort had taken a lot of potential men teachers, there had not been much sports activity. The Agriculture teacher, Arch Yeatts, Jr., had been coaching an intramural baseball team, but inter-school games were limited because of gasoline and teacher shortages. My first year teaching at Climax I decided to start a boys' basketball team using students who had never played the sport and knew very little about it. I think the school furnished the ball, and each student supplied his own pair of black shorts, white T-shirt and shoes. It was a good time for the players and parents. There were one or two with talent for the game, but inexperience in ball-handling and lack of developing planned-play strategy prevented us from winning any games that first year. The girls did not have any sports and wanted a girls' basketball team. There was no woman teacher willing to coach them, so they begged me to be their coach until I consented. The girl's court was divided into three sections with two girls as forwards to shoot goals, one girl in center court to relay the ball between forwards and the two guards at the opposite end of the court from the forwards who tried to block the opposing forwards and to intercept the ball. Because of their and my inexperience, it was a challenging experience for all of us. A few of the girls were really cute making the experience interesting for me.

After establishing my discipline authority during my first year of teaching, my second year resulted in practically no challenges. I encouraged student verbal interchange during class lessons and had no problems keeping these sessions constructive even if not always orderly. With student participation, lessons were more easily learned than the dry lecture-and-test method. I also found that pairing two students, especially in math subjects, to work together on assignments was an effective teaching approach for both the fast and slow paired students. They learned from each other more easily than from an authoritative teacher. The faster student reinforced what she learned by explaining to the slower student who had an incentive to keep up without the possible shame before the teacher and whole class.

My Chemistry class included some laboratory experiments using some chemicals and glass lab ware. The students enjoyed doing these experiments and seeing the results of changing from one substance into something different. I think the lesson involved mixing an acid with a base to make a gas and water when the glass flask of one of the girl students exploded. She was not cut by the glass fragments, but the acid-base liquid splashed onto her face. Students and I washed her face and eyes with lots of water, and she did not appear to be harmed. I could not leave the class, and there was no available emergency service close, so John Rorer, Jr. took her in his car to Doctor Hammer in Chatham. His examination and care found no damage to her. The rest of our laboratory experiments were conducted as a single example with the whole class and me conducting each one as a group.

After my second year of teaching high school, we took a week-end vacation to Fairy Stone State Park near Stuart. It was only about 40 miles away, but the lakeside log cabin gave us a few days of swimming and boating relaxation. We found a few "imperfect" fairy stone crosses.

My second summer working in the cannery started immediately when school ended. Some days were very busy with several customers. Most were home makers preserving excess garden vegetables and a few were with their husbands processing larger amounts of purchased fruits. We furnished folding chairs under oak shade trees for them to do the hand work to get their produce ready for canning. This was a neighborly work-social among women, children and a few men who did not see each other

219

very often. I, too, enjoyed meeting and talking with our customers.

I sold cans and operated the warming tables and pressure cookers to meet temperature and time requirements. Charlie and I both kept sanitary conditions at a high level. Some ladies brought helpers. One helper that I knew at Chatham High School and a friend of Marian's was Sarah Adams. She was a very pretty blond and had a younger brunette sister, Elizabeth, that had been Miss Pittsylvania County. Sarah had been in Florida and was visiting her parents before her plans to go to Richmond to live. We talked awhile, and Charlie suggested that he could handle things if we wanted to "rest" some in his house just behind the cannery. We went to his house where we hugged and kissed a little, but I was very nervous and did not want to go further. Sometime later in the fall I heard that Sarah had gone to Richmond where she had a baby. That information got my attention and brought a lot of thankfulness that I had not gotten involved with her.

Daddy was elected as Board of Directors member, and had been attending regular monthly meetings. The Board decided that the bank needed more capable management so my father was asked to come back to Baltimore as the bank president and chairman of the board of directors. The first time the Bank had one person hold both positions. This was a welcome opportunity for him.

Daddy was in Baltimore at a Director's meeting when mother had us and Katie to Sunday dinner with Paul. Katie, who was working for the County Transportation Department and living in Chatham, often came home on weekends. We were at the table finishing the meal and talking when something was said that upset Paul. He started berating the rest of us and cursing. I told him that he could not talk that way in front of mother and the other women. He became even more infuriated and we both stood up ready to fight and I told him to go outside where we could settle it. Instead, he pushed me into the china cabinet. Mother and Katie intervened before any damage to the furniture or to each other was done.

Marian, Anne and I went home to the cabin. About a week after that, Paul returned to the University of Virginia to finish requirements for his bachelor of arts degree in political science.

My notes:

This action of Paul's was not his usual demonstration of his superiority while still having sympathy for anyone who was in pain or in danger. This was rage that he had not shown before, and I did not recognize at the time. Later in life as old men, he told me that he had to constantly suppress that feeling in order to act as and be a "normally appearing" and productive person. This type of feeling was later described as Post Traumatic Stress Disorder (PTSD).

Daddy and Mother moved to Baltimore and let Marian, Anne and me stay in the home house. Mother had felt sorry for us living in the two-room cabin and made arrangements to have two rooms, a bathroom and a back porch added. I used the mules and a scoop pan to dig a basement to be used as a cellar under the back porch. I laid the concrete blocks for the basement walls, and most of the rest was done by professional builders. I I did the electrical work. During the time that my parents were in Baltimore work on the cabin was finished.

After teaching in the high school for two years, I was offered and accepted a teaching job at Climax for the State Agriculture Department to teach veterans in an on-the-farm training program. That was one of the training programs offered by the government to veterans who wanted a trade or who were not eligible to take advantage of college education. Each veteran was paid $90/month to attend a two-hour class once each week and to work an approved farm crop or project. I received year-round employment at twice my monthly high school teaching salary and was required to teach the class, give farm shop training, plan and conduct field trips and demonstrations and to visit each farm project. This job gave me some free time which allowed me to increase my farming activities.

I think all the students were older than I, but they accepted me as their teacher and mostly were alert during the classes. The oldest was Gerald Reynolds at about 45. He was in one of the last draft groups when the draft pools were getting low on younger men. Larry, his brother, was in the class too. Because he had been Sallie's husband I was a little concerned about how he might react toward me as his teacher. He greeted me in a sincere friendly way and was orderly during the class meetings except for one when he came obviously drunk. I asked him to leave, and he willingly did. After the class ended, I went outside where he was waiting for his ride home with Gerald. I told him I was sorry I had to have him leave, but that I had to have orderly conduct in the class. He apologized and said he was sorry.

Arch Yeatts, Jr. continued as high school Agriculture teacher, and shortly after I started teaching the veteran's class both of us were required to take some 2-week training courses at VPI. I rode with Arch to

Blacksburg, and we both enrolled and got our meal tickets and rooms in the faculty center. My three courses were: Methods in Education, Poultry Methods and Shop. Arch had different classes from mine. The Education classes were rather boring, but I really enjoyed learning about poultry care and shop tools and use.

Marian had taken over the 200 laying-hen flock of White Leghorn's that my mother had. She made some money selling eggs, and used the decorated cotton cloth feed sacks from the store to make dresses and aprons and such. It was a busy time for both of us. We were together in mutually interesting and complementary work that we both enjoyed. I did the field work, and Marian did all the cooking and house work and the light work with the laying hens. We both enjoyed Anne, and Marian visited her mother on her weekly trips to a laundromat in Chatham.

I got a sharecropper, Charlie Gibson and his live-in companion Mrs. Bolling and her two children. Her young boy's name was Clarence, but I do not remember the girl's name. They lived in my tenant house about a half mile from the public road. Mrs. Bolling's older son, Ray, was married to Charlie's daughter. They were sharecroppers on my parent's farm and lived in the tenant house near our home. The two sharecroppers worked together to help each other. I managed the farming and had half interest with my father in a small herd of Aberdeen Angus beef cattle.

With the war over, two of Marian's brothers, John and Taz, came home and were receiving a monthly payment for a limited time while they were looking for employment. John soon was employed at a nuclear processing plant in Oak Ridge, TN, but Taz was lingering at home. Mr. Anderson called me and asked if Taz could live with us and help me on the farm. I agreed to help enroll him in the farm training class and have him stay in the cabin during the week. As part of his training, he would help me on the farm, and he would have meals with us. He was a pleasant guest and a lot of help on the farm during the spring and summer. Marian enjoyed having him for meals, and Taz enjoyed playing with Anne. Taz had itchy feet so in the fall he tried to get back in the Navy, but because they were not accepting enlistments, he joined the Army and was sent to Hawaii.

Henry Carter had been injured during the war and was farming on his father's farm near Chatham. He had graduated with a BS degree in Agriculture from VPI, but he was eligible for the training class at Climax. Henry had been shot in his head, and he said that the shooter was probably one of his own men. He was a hard-driving Captain who was hated by the soldiers he commanded, and he was shot in the back of his head during an intense battle. Henry survived after several surgeries, a metal plate in his skull and a lengthy recovery. He retired as a Major and was still physically and socially active. He said that he was courting a Motley girl that Marian had gone to school with, and he said he had dated Jean Yarboro before she committed suicide. I said that I had known her when we lived in Danville.

When Paul had finished his undergraduate studies, he started to law school at the University of Virginia. Because he did not do well in law school, he came home and found a job teaching History and Civics in the County at Brosville High School. He got room and board with the Estes family in Cascade near the school. Paul and I did not have much communication during his first year of teaching. In June he announced that he and the older Estes girl, Mary Drewry, were getting married. Mother, Daddy, Marian and I went to the wedding ceremony in the Estes house where there were a lot of guests and much celebration. Daddy was Paul's best man and sent the couple off on their honeymoon.

Both Paul and Drewry had quit their teaching jobs at Brosville, and Paul had gotten a job at Planters Bank in Chatham. Marian and I went to visit them for supper in their apartment over the bank. We had a nice time together, and Drewry entertained us with her piano playing. Paul said that she also gave piano lessons to a few students.

I had some tobacco allotment with my 160 acres, and I rented the allotment on my parent's farm using Ray Bolling as the sharecropper. I did not do much work in the tobacco that first year, devoting my work toward the beef cattle, chickens and starting a dairy operation with two cows. I hand milked the cows twice each day and sold the milk in 10-gallon cans as Class C milk to a milk company, Coble, in North Carolina who picked up the full cans from the roadside and returned empties. We got a little extra money from the milk sales, and during the summer unacceptable spoiled milk from a few cans was used to make butter and to feed the liquid to the hogs.

Growing flue-cured bright-leaf tobacco required a lot of hard manual field work. From field preparation with mule-drawn turning plows, harrows, row markers, fertilizer distribution and row listing to the final sale. Tobacco worms were controlled with lead arsenate powder mixed with quick lime and hand-shaken through coarse burlap to dust each plant. This poison was supplemented by hand checking the underside of each leaf and removing and killing any worms found. Instead of traditional hand-picking leaf-axial suckers, a new method of control had been discovered to put a small amount of mineral oil near the top broken-off stalk so that it would flow down into the leaf axials and kill the budding suckers before they had developed enough to rob the plant of nutrition. Our veteran's class visited the Chatham Tobacco Research Station and the Manager, Mr. Matthews, to get demonstrations on this method. I designed and patented an oil nozzle for a hand-operated oil can that applied the oil evenly around the top of the tobacco stalk. The procedure of getting the patent was interesting and required the assistance of a patent attorney. Mr. Mathews tested my prototype and gave a good performance report to me. My invention did not make it to the marketing phase because a new sucker-control chemical spray material was developed that could be applied much easier through a hand or Tractor-drawn sprayer.

Chapter 14

My Way

The mind petrifies if a circle be drawn around it.

George Augustus Moore

I increased my milking-cow herd to 5 cows, hand milked them twice each day and sold the milk in 10-gallon cans as Class C milk to a milk company, Coble, in North Carolina. I cooled the milk in the cabin basement and put the full cans at the roadside where Coble picked them up and returned empties. We got a little extra money from the milk sales, and during the summer unacceptable spoiled milk from a few cans was used to make butter and to feed the liquid to the hogs. Hand-milking 5 cows with large amounts of milk twice daily was slow and time consuming, but it did build a strong hand grip. We did not have electric service at the milking barn to operate a mechanical milking system, so necessity made me think of an inexpensive alternative power source. By then we had a 1947 Chevrolet with manifold-vacuum-operated windshield wipers. I found this vacuum source sufficient to operate one mechanical milker at a time, and plumbed the necessary pipes and tubes to attach the milker.

I drove the car to the milking barn, detached the tube from the manifold-vacuum operated windshield wiper, attached the tube to the milking system and made short work of milking the 5 cows.

Marian and her mother stayed in close contact with visits and phone calls. Marian's brother Sam had not come home after being discharged from the Army, but found work in New Rochelle, NY and married a girl there. Mrs. Anderson and Marian decided to visit him. They rode the bus from Chatham and stayed for about a week visiting and touring that area and New York City. I think Marian had a good time but was glad to be back on the farm with Anne and me.

I got word that Paul had a nervous breakdown and was being treated in the University of Virginia Hospital in Charlottesville. I got further information from our doctor, Cousin Cary Whitehead, and how and where I could go to visit him. When I visited him on a restricted ward, he seemed normal to me but said that he was having trouble being worried, depressed and nervous. When I asked, he thanked me and said that there was nothing I could do to help him. I got in touch with Cary who said that when he found out that Paul had been given electrical shock treatments, he had them discontinued as too much risk for causing permanent brain damage.

My work went on normally, but Paul had major transitions. He did not want to try getting a job in the County, and he did not want to go back to law school at UVA. He and Drewry decided to go to Atlanta, stay with Lou while exploring the possibility of attending Emory University law school. He was accepted and used his veteran's education pay and a part-time job at a Sears store for income. Drewry taught piano lessons.

I don't know how long he and Drewry lived at Lou's terrace apartment, but they had a close relationship. Bobbie was a senior in high school and led an independent life style. From later discussions I found that Paul had tried to intervene in some of her dating relations that backfired into a strained relationship between the two. Don't they ever healed: just a simmering status quo.

After about two years, Paul graduated from Emory Law School, and he and Drewry came to stay with her parents while deciding what to do next.

Some time during their stay in Atlanta, Drewry's mother was killed while parking her car on a hill in Danville. She had not secured the brake before opening the door and getting partly out. Her car rolled back catching her and running over her.

Paul went to Chatham and applied for a Virginia law license, and while he was waiting Judge Langhorn Jones contacted Daddy. Judge Jones asked Daddy if Paul had recovered and was stable enough to practice law. Daddy supported Paul, who was then granted a license. With his reputation, Paul knew he could not get a job as a lawyer in Chatham.

Strained relations with Drewry caused her to seek and get an uncontested divorce. Paul sought refuge and found it with Sallie and her family in Newport News.

Marian and her mother stayed in close contact with visits and phone calls. Marian's brother Sam had not come home after being discharged from the Army, but found work in New Rochelle, NY and married a girl there. Mrs. Anderson and Marian made plans to visit him.

They rode the bus from Chatham and stayed for about a week visiting and touring that area and New York City. I think Marian had a good time but was glad to be back on the farm with Anne and me.

The class program for the veteran's class was not structured with required lesson plans or schedules. I decided what subjects to teach that would apply to the crops and projects of the students and developed my own lesson plans and schedule. I also found places for field trips that would be of interest and value to the class. One place nearby was in Rocky Mount, Virginia where bull semen was collected for use in artificial insemination of cows. The class members who went either rode in two cars or drove their own. I and three students rode with Gerald Reynolds who was formally dressed in a nice suit, a Bowler-type hat and highly polished shoes and drove his new black Buick Roadmaster car. The other students doubled up in a couple more cars. The station manager showed us the facilities and bulls that were semen donors. He then demonstrated the procedure of collecting and testing the samples. He prepared the semen collector by using a piece of plastic pipe 2" diameter by 18" long through which he inserted a longer piece of rubber tubing of the same diameter. The protruding ends of the tubing were folded back over the ends of the pipe and secured tightly with rubber bands. One end of another rubber tube had a glass test tube secured to it, and the open end was secured over one end of the pipe. Warm water was forced through an open valve into the space between the pipe and the internal rubber sleeve until the rubber tube was almost closed along its length. This was the artificial vagina with a sample collecting tube. There were no cows at the station, so a bull was selected as the lure. All bulls had nose rings and were led by poles snapped into the rings. Walkways for the bull and handler were separated by a wooden fence. From preconditioning, all the bulls became excited when one was led to the breeding stall. A technician held the artificial vagina near the tail of the "receiving" bull, and when the donor reared to mount the receiver, the technician placed the artificial vagina in the path of the donor's penis and held it in place for a full penetration. The semen sample was collected in the test tube. Testing for viability of the sperm was done microscopically. A small amount was diluted and placed under a microscope and visually observed for swimming activity.

We also visited commercial dairies and another tobacco research station in Granville County, North Carolina where a tobacco virus disease was being studied. Also, we had a work field day using dynamite to make drainage ditches in a swampy field near the gap in Smith Mountain along Staunton River. After this latter field day did not go as planned, I found out that I should have bought the more sensitive and more nitroglycerin-concentrated dynamite. The concentration we used was not sensitive enough for the initial explosion to set off the next stick in the ditch row. I apologized to the land owner and said we would go back and do the job correctly, but he thanked me and said he would do it later.

I used the left-over dynamite, caps and fuse to blow stumps from a recently cut-over field in my pasture. The stumps were about 18" diameter pine so usually ½ stick was enough to blow each one completely out of the ground and about 6' into the air.

One of my farm visits was to Gerald Reynolds' farm near Hollywood Baptist Church on Gammon Road. I had known Gerald as Larry's brother when Sallie and Larry were married and living on a farm joining Gerald's. Gerald was married to Della then, but they later divorced. Gerald's house on his new farm near Hollywood Baptist Church was down a long driveway from the public road. He was at home preparing breakfast for his present wife and Della who had returned to live with them. The two, present and past, wives worked the 3rd shift at Danville Cotton Mills and would soon be home. After Della divorced Gerald, he married again. Della wanted to return to Gerald, and his second wife agreed, so they both lived happily together with Gerald. Gerald left the breakfast food in the warming oven over the wood-burning cook stove and went with me to a nearby field he was preparing to plant corn. He had two black Buick Roadmaster cars. The one that was several years old, dented and dust-covered was hooked to a disc harrow that he was using to get the field ready for planting, and the other one parked near his house was new, clean and polished. His two "wives" came home while we were in the field and waved to Gerald. His farm projects were up to date, and I left.

Gerald had an older married daughter with small children that were visiting on another visit from me. She and her children really liked Gerald who had a pony for the children to ride. He also had a younger son who lived with him and went to Callands High School. Rumors were that he told his classmates that from his bedroom on the second floor he looked through the floor-board cracks and watched his daddy have sex with one wife and then with the other before they went to sleep with his daddy in the middle.

During these 3 years of farming and teaching the veterans I had farm help from different people and families. Each left looking for a better opportunity. One, Walter Hedrick and his wife went to another farm several miles away. During the late fall he went to a tobacco stripping house to strip the tobacco leaves from the curing sticks and tie them into "hands". Because of the fall early morning cold, he lit the previously laid kindling in a small wood-burning heater. The stove was getting hot when there was a powerful explosion, tearing off one of his legs and blinding his wife. I don't think the person putting dynamite in the heater was ever found. No motive to do harm to Walter was identified, and his family and neighbors thought the harm was directed toward someone else.

Then there was Cabel Carter, a tall muscular single black man about 35 years old who had worked for several farmers in our community and had spent several terms in prison. I had known of him through his marriage to my mother's young servant girl, Mae Nannie Niblet. My father-in-law, Otha Anderson, who was a deputy sheriff as jailer in Chatham, knew I was looking for farm help and called me to tell me that by paying Cabel's fine on a recent infraction he would be available. I think they had discussed this before I received the phone call.

I went to the jail and discussed the situation and procedures with my father in law and a lawyer, Melvin Giles. It was decided that I could not legally hold Cabel to an agreement to work in return for my paying his fine, but we had him sign the paper anyway. I took him home to stay in the empty tenant house on my parent's farm. He ate meals at our house which Marian prepared. During weekends, he stayed with a lady companion and her children not far away.

During the year that Cabel worked for me, we raised the tobacco on my parent's farm, and Charlie and Mrs. Bolling tended the crops on my farm. Cabel did the plowing, tobacco plant bed preparation and other farm labor, and I did the milking and helped with hay harvesting. I was able to hire Cabel's lady friend and family of children to help with the hand work planting tobacco and later with harvesting.

The war-time rationing was over, and new cars and farm machinery were beginning to become available. They were only available by order and a long wait before delivery. Daddy's bank position and association with farmers in Pennsylvania and Maryland resulted in his purchase and delivery of a new Farmall H tractor and some implements.

This addition allowed Cabel and me to increase our acreage of corn, and we added two crops new our farming area, milo and soy beans. Neither of these two crops required cultivation like corn did, and they produced crops that were harvested by labor-saving combine machines.

I would pay Cabel on Fridays after work, and he would return on Monday mornings. Because of his experience working for other neighboring farmers he knew how to do all the farm activities. He was big, strong and farm smart. We got along well for most of the time he worked for me, but toward the middle of the crop season he knew I could not finish the crop without him and took advantage of his position. I would pay him on Fridays as usual, and he would come back on Saturday afternoons partly drunk and ask for an advance on his next week's pay. Don't pay and he might not come back on Monday or pay and he probably would. For me it was never, "to not pay", but to negotiate the minimum he would take to bring him back on Monday morning. I hated to see him on Saturday afternoons but always glad to see him on Monday mornings.

Another field trip with the veteran's class was to the Neuhoff slaughter house in Roanoke. It was the slaughter house that Clyde Brown, the manager of Cundiff's Store, hauled butcher beef cattle to for local farmers. On his return trip, he brought merchandise to sell at the store. As a student group, we were allowed to watch the buying and slaughter process. The cattle to be slaughtered and butchered were herded from the holding lot into a single-file fenced lane to the killing station inside. Instead of a rifle that most of us used at our home hog killing, there was a head stanchion to hold each cow's head still and a hefty man holding a sledge hammer standing on a platform next to and higher than the cow.

After a cow's neck was clamped in the stanchion, the sledge hammer was swung to hit the cow in the head between the eyes. The stanchion was released as the cow dropped, and another man attached an electrically operated winch to the back legs and pulled the carcass up and along a ceiling-mounted track. The next station was for bleeding and skinning, and the next one was where the hide was removed, the abdomen opened, entrails removed for cleaning and all edible parts for humans separated. The final processing station was over a butchering table where the remaining carcass was cut into quarters and hung in a walk-in cooler for storage. It appeared that all parts would be used for human or animal food. The hides were gathered in bundles and hauled to the tannery a few miles away in Salem. The odor for miles around the tannery was putrid and strong enough to make a person sick. We did not go there.

When I did not have work for Cabel in the crops, we built and repaired fences and cut trees for pulp, lumber and veneer. We used a two-man cross-cut saw to fell the trees and cut the logs to the desired lengths. The limbs were cut off using axes. By then I had sold my model A Ford and bought a civilian model Jeep which I used to pull the logs on a four-wheel, rubber-tired wagon. The pine pulp wood had to be cut into 8-foot lengths and then stacked in box cars at the Chatham railway freight station. Cabel was physically suited for that kind of work, but I soon learned that I was not.

Our experience with veneer logs was a little less physically demanding, and the sale price was higher. We cut large tulip poplar trees into the 8-foot lengths required by the veneer factory in Ferrum, VA about40 miles west, loaded them onto the wagon using skid poles and cant hooks and hauled them to Ferrum. Except for tire replacement costs, this was more rewarding and less strenuous work.

We cut a few trees for lumber to build shelters. These were taken to a sawmill about 7 miles away for custom sawing. This small sawmill was owned and operated by Jessee Ramsey who previously used part of his property for a blacksmith and farrier shop near Bearskin Creek. When I was about ten and twelve years old, I rode our mules there to have new shoes put on their front hooves. I remember they were long, painful, bareback rides on raw-boned mules.

With the need to spend more time in harvesting crops, we quit the logging activities. I sold the standing pine timber to Mr. Bates from Mountain Valley near Martinsville for a set price. He moved his sawmill to my farm to cut and saw the trees into lumber. I used the money to pay my Daddy toward his loan to me.

I got more involved with farming and was not spending as much time as I should with teaching and farm visits, and the state office was getting more organized in managing the veteran farm training program. For my first two years I had very little supervision except for written monthly reports and an occasional announced visit by the program manager. By the third year, an area supervisor was assigned to make unannounced visits. One time he found me with Cable in my hay field getting up hay. He did not seem displeased about my personal work, but I felt uncomfortable. I started making a few more farm project visits and took more time preparing lessons.

My visit to Enoch Osborne's was after lunch on a hot day. I parked at the end of his driveway and as I was walking toward his house I shouted, "Hello" as was the custom when no one was in sight. Two big hound dogs sprung from under his front porch, barking, growling with teeth bared and feet clawing earth coming for me. I knew better than to run, so I stood still and started talking at the dogs. Enoch came out of his house and called to his dogs. They stopped and started walking back to the house. I talked with Enoch about his project, and we went to see the status of his fields. I checked off my visit and left, but I had the truth of the adage, "Leave sleeping dogs lie" reinforced.

Daddy had worked as a federal government employee at the Federal Land Bank long enough and was old enough to retire with a livable pension. He and Mother moved back to Windcrest, and Marian, Anne and I moved into the expanded cabin.

Sometimes I became disappointed with our sex infrequency, but I did not know how to discuss my feelings. Sex was not an easy subject for me. It was an overwhelming influence that drove my life, and which I was not able to admit for fear of exposing a weakness. It was like the Holy Grail, Golden Chalice, Unspeakable Holiness that demanded averting my eyes as in fear of HOLY GOD. I just could not talk about it. Marian certainly did not have the desire near equal to mine, and she did not talk about it either. I started to understand Coach French's encounter with the girl in Staunton, but I was not thinking about following his example. I wanted to solve my own problem with Marian, and I seemed incapable of finding a way.

On my way to milk one morning, I thought about the cow-stump jokes I had heard and decided to try relieving my lust using the small Angus-Guernsey cross cow. After putting feed in the hay rack and feed trough, I started the milker on the first cow and unzipped my pants and took my erected penis out behind the small cow. I was attempting to put my penis in her genital when I saw shadows across spaces in the vertical -board siding. Someone was moving just outside the cow shed. I zipped my pants closed before Daddy said something and opened the door. I was startled, but continued with my milking and answered his question, "Do you need any help" with "No." He then left without saying anything else. If he saw me doing anything other than normal milking activity, he never mentioned it. I did not make any other attempt to test the cow-stump tale. I did wonder though why he came to the cow shed.

The uncertain relationship with Cabel continued through the tobacco harvest until the final leaves were in the curing barn. On the following Monday morning Cabel did not come, and he did not come on Tuesday either. I think it was Wednesday when my father-in-law called and told Marian that Cabel was found dead in some woods on the other side of the county near his sister's house. He had become violent and threatening there and, while wielding a knife, chased his sister's husband around and through their house. On the last trip through the house the husband grabbed a loaded shotgun and shot Cabel as he came out of the house. Cabel ran away down a hill into the woods. The husband did not follow and did not know until later that Cabel had died .

The sheriff's department investigated but did not prosecute the husband. Cabel's sister came and asked for money to pay for his burial. He was already in debt to me for over $200 so I did not contribute. I think my sister Katie gave her some money. Having no help after Cabel died, I worked long hours getting crops harvested and the last curing of tobacco moved into the pack house.

On Sunday morning, the tobacco in the curing barn close alongside the public road had become flexible enough to move to the pack barn up the road across from Windcrest. I had stopped attending church at Greenpond and used that time to do farm work, so I was getting the sticks of tobacco down from the tier poles in the barn onto the farm wagon when Daddy came and gave an emotional talk about how he had spent his life trying to establish a good name in the community and my working on Sunday in a place in view of passing traffic was destroying what he had done. He was devastated as he walked back home. My Daddy chastised me for working on Sunday because it would give our family a bad name for breaking the Sabbath. He was very sensitive about his family's reputation in the community. His father had been a drunkard, drug addict, general loafer and womanizer. His father's membership in Greenpond Baptist Church was finally revoked, and his mother had resigned her membership in disgrace and support of her husband. Daddy had spent his life trying to rebuild trust in his family's reputation and was very protective of his good name. I felt awful and yet frustrated that I was expected to walk in his shadow as he demanded. I had to leave, and my asthma, while being enough to cause me to go, may not have been the major reason.

I had not been bothered by asthma while going to college in Blacksburg and decided to get relief there and get a master's degree in Industrial Physics. I resigned from my teaching job and concentrated on getting ready to leave the farm and move to Blacksburg.

I finished getting the tobacco from the curing barn to the pack barn by myself. My Daddy chastised me for working on Sunday because it would give our family a bad name for breaking the Sabbath. He was very sensitive about his family's reputation in the community. His father had been a drunkard, drug addict, general loafer and womanizer. His membership in Greenpond Baptist Church was finally revoked. My Daddy had spent his life trying to rebuild trust in his family's reputation and was very protective of his good name.

I had been a chronic asthmatic since early childhood with sporadic acute attacks. During that year I had been especially affected by dust from hay, chickens and other sources and from various pollens which I had been self-treating with adrenaline injections. I had thoughts of giving up farming and devoting more effort to my teaching job, but this incident with Daddy convinced me that I could not live the life he wanted me to. I had seen the effect he had on Sallie and Paul and knew that I would need to get away from his daily influence. To stay would result in a confrontation because I could not live the life he wanted me to.

My announced reason for leaving was to get relief from asthma by going back to college in Blacksburg where I had not been bothered by asthma.

I went to VPI and talked with the Dean of the Physics Department, Dr. Robeson, about getting am MS degree in Industrial Physics. My undergraduate courses would be acceptable for a lot of my credits, but because I would need to take some undergraduate courses in order to take the graduate ones, it would take me two years instead of the usual one year.

I told Marian what I intended to do, and she agreed. I gave notice to the School Board and started getting my farm business liquidated.

I still owed Daddy on the farm loan he had given me, so I offered to sell my interests to him at the price he had sold it to me. There were some adjustments for the timber sales that I paid to him and some improvements that I had made. He also bought my interests in the beef cattle and hogs.

Clyde Brown hauled my dairy cows to the livestock market in Roanoke, and I got Moses Gibson to finish preparing my tobacco for sale. Marian and I went to Blacksburg and rented an apartment in a four-apartment house at 312 Main Street across the street from the entrance to the college campus. Clyde Brown moved our furniture and a lot of canned and frozen food in his cattle truck.

Chapter 15

Blacksburg

An intelligent hell would be better than a stupid paradise.

Victor Hugo's play "Ninety-three"

To leave the farm required a lot of preparation and divesting of the farm, farm animals and equipment.

I resigned from my teaching job and arranged to keep the health insurance under a private policy. A new teacher was found with no interruption in the classes. One of the students bought my best Holstein milk cow, and I sold the others at the livestock market in Roanoke.

I had finished harvesting tobacco, but had not prepared it for market. I paid a neighbor farmer, Moses Gibson, to get it ready so Daddy could take it to market in Danville for me.

I had harvested and sold all my corn and soy beans, and Marian churned a lot of butter, canned a lot of vegetables and froze some chicken and pork.

My asthma attacks had been getting more frequent and severe during the summer of 1950. The only relief was with injections of adrenaline which were only available from a physician. My cousin, Cary Whitehead, was our physician and knew my character and reliability to be trustworthy so he gave me unlimited prescriptions for adrenaline, hypodermic syringes and needles so I would not have to go to a physician or an emergency room for relief.

Our five years of marriage at Climax on the farm had been a trusting, loving partnership of mutual family work as a social relationship between us, our families and neighbors. We were in a community familiar to and loved by us. There were very few strangers to us, and we could always find and give help and friendship as normal life.

I think Marian was happy with Anne and her life on the farm. She was a liked and respected member of an extended community and was contributing to her family and the community. She had a desire to express her own personality and took a correspondence course in painting which she enjoyed and in which she showed some talent. She obtained from a neighbor a small, short-haired, tan and black Fox Terrier-Manchester cross female dog that looked like a miniature Manchester. Marian named her "Winkle". She and Anne then had a personal friend that gave them much pleasure. Winkle was spayed, immunized and licensed and was one of our family.

I usually was busy working either on the farm or with students and did not take much time for entertainment. Marian worked a lot too with house and farm work, but she liked to include some jokes and silly things as part of our daily life. Each day was about the same for me, but Marian looked forward to making a special event on holidays.

I had just recently bought a prime registered Spotted Poland China boar from a neighbor, Lewis Gregory, that I wanted to use to upgrade the quality of my hogs and to furnish stud service to other nearby farmers. One morning when I was nearly finished milking, Marian came running to the milking barn and shouted very excitedly, "Come quick, the new boar is choking and has fallen down and is kicking his legs". I quit what I was doing and ran with her to the hog lot to find Cabel there looking very serious and nothing wrong with the boar. She broke out in convulsive laughing saying, "April Fool, April Fool". Cabel laughed a lot too. I was not happy and felt like I would enjoy giving her a good spanking.

For one Easter, Marian brought home two baby ducklings for Anne. The ducklings attached to Anne as a surrogate mother and followed her as they would a mother duck. They would swim in a large wash tub of water and peep in apparent joy. We were told that if they were turned on their back they could not right themselves, would not make much effort to do so and just give up and die. One did when it was not watched closely enough. I don't remember what happened to the other one.

We used woven "rat" wire to protect grain and animal feed from mice and large wharf rats, but the spillage and cracks around doors allowed some rats to enter the hen and feed houses. The loss of feed was not large, but Marian hated having rats scurrying around where she was tending the hens and hogs. Occasionally I would shoot one using my 22 caliber rifle or Daddy's 12-gauge shotgun, but Marian wanted me to do more. It took time to get in position and wait for a rat to show itself, and we were busy in tobacco harvest so her requests were not satisfied. Cabel, his lady companion, her children and I were across the road under the shade of oak trees tying harvested leaves on tobacco sticks when we heard a shotgun blast. Shortly after that, Marian came along the driveway toward us with a big smile on her face carrying the shotgun in one hand and a large rat by its tail in the other. She said, "That's how it's done" and turned back toward the house. Cabel's lady friend said, "Lord God a'mighty, it's a wonder that big gun didn't knock her down."

Our community social life was mostly with the church, school or Ruritan Club. The church was mostly Sunday services, but during the summer we had revival services nightly for a week. To end the revival, we had a church picnic and home coming the last Sunday afternoon. Family members who had moved away came, and local members who did not attend Sunday service regularly came for the picnic. The women prepared the food and enjoyed many compliments on their cooking skills. Children ran wild under the trees and around the church but not inside the "Sacred" church building. Adults were dressed in their "finest" and enjoyed telling and hearing local news and gossip.

The school had sports games and an occasional musical event with a name country band. We also put on a highly advertised and anticipated "Woman-less Wedding" featuring some of the most burly and masculine farmers as "ladies".

The all-men Ruritan Club held monthly dinner meetings in the school cafeteria. Wives prepared and served the meals during which they enjoyed social interchanges. Marian enjoyed these outings and especially the one celebrating April Fools by serving biscuits each made with a ball of cotton stuffed inside. The wives watched as the men tried to eat the biscuits in a way to not show any impoliteness. The wives could not contain themselves and came from the kitchen laughing and shouting, "April Fool."

Marse Ferrell finished college and had worked for a chemical company in Louisiana. He met and married a niece of Hughey Long, a former famous governor and US senator from Louisiana. Marse gave up that job and returned with his wife to live at home and work in Dan River Mills.

We were only living a "subsistence life" economically, and I don't think we realized what a full and relatively happy life we were leaving in my search of relief from asthma, financial security and independent status. We all paid a big price with Marian paying the most.

We moved to Blacksburg to start my graduate education in Industrial Physics. A local store owner, Clyde Brown, who had been hauling my cattle to market at the Neuhoff Slaughter House in Roanoke moved all our belongings including a lot of food supplies on his cattle truck. He parked his truck on the hill in front of our new residence at 312 North Main Street to unload the overflowing cattle truck. During the unloading process, one of the bags of potatoes came open letting a flood of potatoes roll down the street. It took us some time to gather them. We had enough frozen food, potatoes and canned goods to supply most of our food for over a year. When I sold my cattle, tobacco, farm animals and crops, we had enough money to pay living expenses and tuition at Virginia Tech. It was many, many years after that before I had enough money to last more than a month between paydays.

Marian, Anne and I lived in a three-room and bath first-floor apartment in a large four-apartment house across from the campus. There was a fenced back yard where we made a place for Winkle and for Anne to play. We could store our potatoes and canned goods in the basement, and our frozen pork, chicken and butter in a freezer locker place in Christiansburg a few miles away. It was a familiar place for me, but a new one for Marian and Anne.

Until we moved to Blacksburg, Marian had only lived in the Chatham area where she had close relatives and friends. We did not know anyone here so it was a big adjustment for her and Anne. Our church attendance gave us a social outing on Sunday mornings, but it did not develop into any personal friendship. Our entertainment was meager and consisted of an occasional movie and walking around the campus. Color photography had just become available to the public. It was expensive, but I splurged and bought a roll of color film so I could take some pictures of Marian and Anne. They were beautiful in the resulting pictures. The campus had been there a long time, and the architectural differences between the buildings were an interesting demonstration of style changes and enrollment growth. The older, original red brick buildings of the upper quadrangle contrasted with the newer gray stone buildings around the drill field. Visiting the upper quadrangle and seeing the K Battery barracks where I spent two years in the military as an undergraduate made me glad those days of torment were over. The word "Haze" was not used to describe the torture freshmen were given for a full year as "Rats." It was called "Military Discipline." I told Marian about my experiences in that building.

I told Marian of these and some other undergraduate experiences I had and how my nonacademic life was so much better with her. One Sunday we drove about 20 miles through the Jefferson National Park and up a mountain side to Mountain Lake. We enjoyed the mountain scenery and the crystal-clear water of the lake at the top.

Marian became friends with the wife of another student who lived in the apartment across the dividing hall in our house. This gave her some social contact, but they, like us, were on a subsistence budget. From some of Marian's new approaches to sex, I thing they talked some about that. I did not encourage her enough in her new interest in sexual activity, and it soon passed. This was not my first or last unintentional error of ignorance, but it spread through time and people like the ripples from a stone thrown into still water to cause devastating effects on many people as well as on me.

Because I was in a new curriculum of physics instead of biology in which I got my bachelor's degree, I had to take extra pre-required subjects and work very hard to make good grades. We still had our "47 Chevrolet 4-door, but because of restricted parking on campus I walked to classes. After a quarter or two, Marian saw an opportunity for her to try college education. Tuition was not expensive at that time, and I encouraged her. She signed up for an English class being taught by my cousin, Reginald, "Duke", Kenny, who had also taught me English at Hargrave in Chatham. He was a strict and demanding teacher, and Marian struggled to get passing grades. Anne, who was 4 at that time, was left at a daycare place during her classes.

Because we were not using our car, I decided to sell it and buy a vacuum cleaner and an automatic dishwasher to give Marian a little more time with her studies. It did not help much, and later I wished that I had given her something else less expensive and kept the car.

The first year in Blacksburg was mostly my adjusting to being a student again and Marian adjusting without family nearby. My social life was satisfied through daily classes, but Marian was limited to wives in the other apartments and the students in her one English class. She did have some contacts with other mothers at Anne's day care. I think we went to church most Sundays, but I don't remember any church or other social activities there. We were trying to make our money last until my graduation and a new job, so our entertainment expenditures were almost non-existent. I don't remember our considering Marian getting a job.

Our life in Blacksburg was drastically different from our previous five years on the farm where we worked together as a team. I had teaching and farm work, and Marian had farm work and food preparation and preservation. We each needed the other for help which required communication and cooperation as a social activity. Here each was doing things more as an individual not requiring as much dependence or help from the other. I was intensely involved in school work which was not shared with Marian, and she had no planned activity outside the home. There was no outward conflict between us, just an acceptance with no real joy of joint accomplishment. I don't think we adjusted well to this new way of living.

The only family social contact I can remember other than an occasional movie was a dinner guest of my cousin, "Duke" Kenny. He was rotund with a rosy complexion and wore silver round-rimmed spectacles giving the stereotypical appearance of an intellectual Englishman. We talked some about Chatham and relatives there, but the most enjoyable part of the evening for us was his description of his visit to the 10,000-acre ranch of my cousin and his brother-in-law, Richard Whitehead, in Arizona. The telling of his apprehension in a totally strange environment among Native Americans in their every-day clothes set a very humorous tone at our dinner table. He was a very entertaining person whom we enjoyed.

A second year was required for me to get a Master's degree, so our finances became a controlling influence on our life style. One of my physics teachers, Dr. Loh, got an assistant job for me to grade papers for him at a salary of $100/month which was a big help. During the fall of 1951, Marian became pregnant. She did not suffer morning sickness as severe or as long as she had during her pregnancy with Anne. I suffered much less with asthma attacks, and except for getting two impacted wisdom teeth extracted, we stayed healthy with few medical expenses. My dwindling financial resources and the new baby on the way put more pressure on me to find a job as soon as possible after graduation.

My course work became more difficult for me. I was taking Graduate Math, X-ray Crystal Structure and Theoretical Physics, the latter of which I had serious trouble with. I found that I am good at things I can visualize or physically handle, but am not as good at understanding or working with theoretical concepts. I chose my thesis to build and calibrate an optical-electronic instrument with Professor Ryan as my adviser. It was good enough to get a grade of B, and my grades of C in graduate math and theoretical physics were stretched by sympathetic professors. I did pass my comprehensive examination and was given a Master's in Industrial Physics in May of 1952. Lou was visiting Mother and Daddy at that time, and all three came to my graduation. It was a happy event and a short reunion.

A campus visit in March by a job recruiter, Harold Forstat, from the Army Biological Warfare Laboratories at Fort Detrick, Maryland resulted in my being offered a job there to start in June. I was to be employed by the federal government at their pay scale and professional grade. I was to be a GS-7 at $4,700/year, but I first had to get a Top Secret clearance from the FBI. This would take time, and then there was time required to get final personnel approval for a start date. I finished my graduate work toward the end of April and was assured through phone and mail that my job was waiting, but final approval for a start date had not been given by Army Personnel. I had no other prospects of a job, and I really wanted the one at Fort Detrick. Marian went by bus to Frederick to find a place for us to live. It was at 255 Church Street, the first floor of a residence on the corner of Church and North Bentz Streets across from Baker Park. It had a fenced back yard suitable for Anne and Winkle. We had a moving company move us this time at a fixed price. Marian, Anne, Winkle and I took the bus to Frederick and were waiting for the movers when they arrived.

Epilogue

My life experiences and, I think, no one else's in the generations I knew ever received the kind of education described by Erich Fromm in the Chapter 12 heading. It was mostly "Do the best you can. Obey your father and mother. Spare the rod and spoil the child. This is the way my mother raised me, and that is the way I'm going to raise mine." All admonitions to continue past errors.

A few more errors of ignorance and non cognitively recallable shaming memories result in an ever increasing deviation from the path of true love and happiness; individual and social.

My Daddy carried an unrecognized burden which had the most effect on his children. He expected all of them to be the kind of public example that would erase the kind of life and reputation of his father. He set strict guides, and he furnished material and education for them to use as an aid in their effort.

Daddy was a personal part of my early and young adult life only a few times. The year I lived in Baltimore as a high-school sophomore he took me along with two other Federal Land Bank employees to a business meeting in Dover, Delaware. I was an observer, but very much a part of his group. Also, during that year he went with me to a parent's meeting at City College and made the rounds of my classes and teachers. My Daddy had a charming personality and seemed to be genuinely interest in how I was doing.

Other than those and maybe a few more times he never discussed any part of my life except discipline and behavior. Not even what college I chose to go to or the subject I chose to major in. Just that I went and graduated. All paid for with no question or hesitation. I am grateful for all of that. I never emotionally missed Daddy or wished for more personal time from him. He was not there, and I did not have any other life experiences for comparison.

One regret I do have about having him as a father is the lack of trying to teach me more about sex instead of leaving me to learn from inadequate observation of farm and pet animals and other children. That one kind of information would have helped let me make my life and my romantic associates less stressful.

The rest of my early and early adult life was just learning to become a physical and psychological person. This learning process encompassed a wide variety of locations, experiences and social contacts and environments from which I became the person I am.

Part 2 will continue this trail of errors of ignorance.

Made in the USA
Columbia, SC
19 May 2021